Last-Minute

TRAVEL

SECRETS

JOEY GREEN

121 INGENIOUS TIPS

TO ENDURE CRAMPED PLANES, CAR TROUBLE, AWFUL HOTELS, AND OTHER TRIPS FROM HELL

CHICAGO REVIEW PRESS

The author has conducted all the travel secrets in this book and has made every reasonable effort to ensure that the travel secrets are safe when conducted as instructed. However, neither the author nor the publisher assumes any liability for damages caused or injury sustained from conducting these travel secrets.

A responsible adult should supervise any young reader who conducts the travel secrets in this book to avoid potential danger or injury.

Published by Chicago Review Press Incorporated
814 North Franklin Street
Chicago, Illinois 60610
ISBN 978-1-61373-504-6

Library of Congress Cataloging-in-Publication Data
Names: Green, Joey, author.
Title: Last-minute travel secrets : 121 ingenious tips to endure cramped
    planes, car trouble, awful hotels, and other trips from Hell / Joey Green.
Description: Chicago, Illinois : Chicago Review Press, 2016. | Includes
    bibliographical references.
Identifiers: LCCN 2015049814 (print) | LCCN 2016004778 (ebook) | ISBN
    9781613735046 (paperback) | ISBN 9781613735053 (PDF edition) | ISBN
    9781613735077 (EPUB edition) | ISBN 9781613735060 (Kindle edition)
Subjects: LCSH: Travel—Miscellanea. | BISAC: TRAVEL / Reference. | REFERENCE
    / Handbooks & Manuals.
Classification: LCC G151 .G735 2016 (print) | LCC G151 (ebook) | DDC 910—dc23 LC record
    available at http://lccn.loc.gov/2015049814

Cover and interior design: Andrew Brozyna, AJB Design Inc.
Cover and interior layout: Jonathan Hahn

Printed in the United States of America
5 4 3 2 1

"Love many, trust few, and learn to paddle your own canoe."

—Unknown

CONTENTS

3 HOTELS AND HOVELS 55

Introduction

When my wife, Debbie, and I backpacked around the world for two years on our honeymoon, we learned to travel with two aerosol cans in our backpacks: disinfectant, to freshen the air in the musty hotel rooms, train compartments, and ship cabins; and insecticide, to ward off any six-legged pests.

One night, after a 10-hour bus ride across the Indonesian island of Flores, we checked into the last available room in Hotel Lila Graha, a dismal budget inn that our guidebook called "the saving grace of the town." Debbie immediately misted the room with disinfectant, and I sprayed insecticide under the two single beds and into the drain in the middle of the bare concrete floor in the bathroom. We went out for dinner, and upon returning to the room, Debbie opened the bathroom door, flicked on the light, and discovered more than 30 cockroaches flipped on their backs across the floor, some dead, others flailing their legs. How could we possibly sleep in this room?

We pushed the two beds together in the center of the room and set up our self-standing igloo tent on top of the mattresses so we could sleep inside it, elevated from the floor, in the comfort of our own sleeping bags.

While our night in Indonesia might seem extreme, nothing tests your ability to live by your wits like travel. Even if you're traveling just for the weekend to a resort hotel, you'll still be confronted by unexpected challenges. But with a little ingenuity and resourcefulness, you can put everyday items to use in unconventional ways to prevail over any unforeseen travel contingency, like how to find your car in a parking lot with a water bottle, fix a broken luggage wheel with duct tape, and incapacitate a hijacker with a pot of coffee.

In this book, you'll discover how to make a pair of slippers from maxi pads, improvise noise-canceling headphones with a tennis ball, and seal hotel curtains shut with clothes hangers. You'll find step-by-step instructions on how to waterproof a map with hairspray, store valuables in a shaving cream can, and lock a suitcase with a paper clip. You'll learn how to hide valuables in a comfy chair, turn a trash can into a toilet with a pool noodle, grease a car axle with vegetable oil, uncork a wine bottle with a sneaker, and heat up a frozen TV dinner on a car manifold.

How did I come up with these unorthodox travel secrets? While backpacking around the world, Debbie and I repaired the mosquito netting on our tent door with dental floss. During our seven-day train journey from Moscow to Beijing aboard the Trans-Siberian express, I mastered the art of giving myself a shower using a water bottle. While hiking through the Andes Mountains in Peru, we lubricated the zippers on our sleeping bags with lip balm. While driving across the United States, I cleaned our cloudy headlights with toothpaste and scraped ice from the windshield with a spatula. We've snuck liquor aboard a cruise ship using food coloring and an empty mouthwash bottle. While driving an RV down the east coast of Australia, we cleaned road grime from the windshield with a can of Coca-Cola. I've insulated camper windows with Bubble Wrap, washed my clothes with a salad spinner, kept toilet paper dry with a CD spindle, silenced a dripping sink in a creepy hotel room with dental floss, dried wet hiking boots with newspaper, improvised earplugs with tampons, and slept in a corner of an airport waiting area with a newspaper. When the going gets tough, the tough get inventive. As Teddy Roosevelt said, "When you're at the end of your rope, tie a knot and hold on."

Incidentally, we never informed the Indonesian hotel owner about the swarm of dead cockroaches on the bathroom floor. When we checked out the next morning, Debbie noticed a teenage houseboy entering our room to clean it. Perturbed, he fetched the owner to show him the murder scene. The owner merely shrugged his shoulders and nonchalantly returned to the front desk of "the saving grace of the town."

1

PACKING TRICKS

While preparing to travel to the Amazon jungle, I asked a Vietnamese emigrant working in a camping store in New York City if the store sold mosquito nets.

"Buy it when you get there," he advised.

"But what if they don't sell mosquito nets in the Amazon?"

He laughed. "Believe me," he said, "the people in the Amazon don't like mosquitoes any more than you do."

How to Store Valuables in a Shaving Cream Can

WHAT YOU NEED

- Safety goggles
- Can of shaving cream, 10 ounces
- Work gloves
- Safety can opener
- Water
- Sandpaper, 220 grit
- Scissors
- Hot glue gun
- PVC coupling, 1½-inch ABS DWV H × H
- Sheet of foam rubber with adhesive backing

WHAT TO DO

1. Wearing safety goggles, empty the shaving cream and as much pressurized gas as possible from the shaving cream can by pressing the nozzle until the can is completely empty. ***Do not attempt to cut into the can if it contains shaving cream***, otherwise the pressurized can may explode, producing metal shrapnel.

2. Wearing safety goggles and work gloves, and working outdoors, use the safety can opener to carefully open the bottom of the empty shaving cream can. Make the initial puncture at the back of the can, in case the can opener makes a small dent in the metal. When you first puncture the can, the remaining pressurized gas in the can may squirt a small amount of shaving cream from the hole.

3. Carefully rinse out the can with water, ***being careful not to cut yourself*** on the sharp bottom edge.

4. Wearing work gloves, lightly sand the bottom edge with 220-grit sandpaper—without grazing the paint on the side of the can.

5. Using a pair of scissors, snip off the plastic tube from inside the can as close to the top of the can as possible.

6. Using the hot glue gun, attach the piece of PVC coupling (with the factory-cut edge facing down to ensure a precise fit) onto the inside of the can bottom.

7. Cut several strips of foam rubber 1 inch wide and adhere them inside the circumference of the can, roughly ¼ inch above the bottom edge as shown, to create a ring of foam so the plastic tube attached to the bottom lid fits snugly inside.

8. Place money or valuables inside the can, replace the bottom lid, and stand the can on a shelf in your medicine cabinet. To prevent jewelry from jangling inside the can, wrap the items in a tissue before placing them inside the can.

HOW IT WORKS

The plastic tube attached to the bottom lid fits snugly inside the ring of adhesive foam attached to the inner wall of the empty shaving cream can, allowing you to hide anything that fits inside the hollow can.

HUSH MONEY

In the 1993 movie *Jurassic Park*, computer programmer Dennis Nedry (Wayne Knight) uses a modified Barbasol shaving cream can to smuggle frozen dinosaur embryos from Jurassic Park on Isla Nublar. Nedry crashes his jeep, drops the can (which gets covered by mud), and gets killed by a Dilophosaurus. The fate of the Barbasol cryocan provides the main storyline for *Jurassic Park: The Game*.

OFF THE BEATEN TRACK

How to Pack Light

- Choose a small bag, which automatically prevents you from taking more than fits in the bag.
- Pack clothes for no more than seven days. Wash your laundry once a week rather than carrying the weight of additional garments.
- Abide by the travelers' maxim "Lay out only what you absolutely need. Then take half the clothes and twice the money."
- Roll your clothes, rather than folding them, to maximize the space in your luggage.

- Stuff socks inside your shoes to maximize space and prevent the shoes from crushing.
- Stack bras on top of each other, fold them in half, and stuff underwear inside the cavity. This method helps bras maintain their shape, extends the life of the undergarments, and saves space.

- Pack a pair of shoes inside a shower cap to prevent the soles from dirtying your clothes.
- Place bottles of shampoo and conditioner inside your shoes to prevent both the bottles and shoes from crushing.
- Avoid packing toiletry items you can buy at your destination.
- Pack items that can serve several purposes, such as a bandana and a sarong.
- Pack a can opener, some plastic silverware, and a can of tuna fish. If you arrive late at your destination with no place open to buy food, you'll have emergency rations.

- Wear your bulkier items, such as boots, a sweater, and a jacket.

How to Organize Clothes with Ziplock Freezer Bags

WHAT YOU NEED

- Ziplock freezer bags, 1-gallon or 2-gallon size
- Plastic drinking straw (optional)

WHAT TO DO

1. Pack clothes for one outfit (especially for children) into a freezer bag, zip the bag shut most of the way (leaving an opening roughly 1 inch long), and then sit on the bag to expel the air.
2. Place your mouth against the opening and inhale to suck the remaining air from the bag. Or insert a plastic drinking straw through the opening and into the center of the plastic bag, seal the bag shut (up to the straw), suck out the air from the bag, and pull out the straw.
3. Zip the bag shut, and pack it in your suitcase.

HOW IT WORKS

The plastic freezer bags contain the clothes, making it easier to stay organized, and sucking the air from the bags compresses the amount of space the clothes take up.

OFF THE BEATEN TRACK

16 Must-Pack Items

- **Bandana.** The multipurpose cloth can be used as a scarf, headband, bandage, place mat, hand towel, potholder . . . the list seems endless.
- **Duct Tape.** Carry a small roll to repair luggage, shoes, tents, and guidebooks, and to seal boxes.
- **Earplugs.** These lifesavers help buffer you against screaming babies or snoring roommates.
- **Emergency Medical Kit.** Don't forget to pack your medications and first aid equipment (bandages, antibiotic ointment, etc.) in a small zippered bag.
- **Eye Mask.** It's lightweight and helps keep the light out so you can get shut-eye on a plane, train, bus, or inside a cheap hotel room with a neon light flashing outside the window.

- **Flashlight.** A small LCD pocket light comes in handy at night for illuminating dark paths or passages, finding the bathroom, and reading books or maps.
- **Flip-Flops.** Wear them in the shower at hotels and hostels to avoid getting athlete's foot or plantar warts.

- **Pillowcase and/or Sheet.** If you get stuck somewhere with questionable bedding, having your own pillowcase and sheet helps you rest easy.
- **Power Strip.** If the airport lounge lacks outlets, you can turn a single outlet into a public outlet.
- **Rope.** A 6-foot length of rope comes in handy as a clothesline.

- **Safety Pins.** These indispensible tools can replace missing buttons, substitute for zipper pulls, and clasp together the zippers of your daypack to thwart thieves.
- **Single-Load Detergent Packet.** Keep a box of laundry detergent in a ziplock bag, or empty the powder into the bag to conserve space. You'll need this to wash your clothes in a sink.
- **Tote Bag.** Great as a carry-on bag, grocery bag, picnic bag, or beach bag.
- **Towel.** You'll need this at hostels and beaches. A microfiber towel takes up less space in your bag and dries quicker than a conventional towel.
- **Universal Sink Stopper.** If you plan to wash your clothes in any sinks, have one of these to make sure you can stop the drain.
- **Ziplock Bags.** These resealable waterproof bags can hold food, jewelry, or powdered laundry detergent.

How to Protect Jewelry with Buttons and a Pill Container

WHAT YOU NEED

- Medium-sized buttons
- Day-of-the-week pill container
- Tissues
- Rubber bands (or elastic hair bands)
- Ziplock freezer bag

WHAT TO DO

1. Remove the back from a pair of stud earrings, poke the two pins in opposite holes in the button, and replace the backs on the pins from the underside of the button to hold the pair of earrings in place.
2. Place a different piece of jewelry inside each compartment of the pill container.
3. Crumple up tissues and place one in each compartment to prevent the jewelry from jangling around while traveling.
4. Seal the pill container shut, and wrap a rubber band around it lengthwise for added security.
5. Slip the pill container into the ziplock bag and seal it. This way, should the pill container pop open unexpectedly, the bag will catch any jewelry that may fall out.
6. Place the pill container flat in the suitcase between layers of clothing to prevent it from opening unexpectedly.

HOW IT WORKS

The buttons keep the pairs of earrings together and prevent them from getting lost, and the pill container keeps the jewelry organized, sorted, and tangle-free. The pill container provides seven compartments for you to pack enough jewelry for a weeklong trip.

EVERY TRICK IN THE BOOK

Happy Pills

Pill containers have a wide variety of other convenient uses:

- **Craft Container.** Store beads and pins in a weekly pill container (at half the price of craft storage boxes). With the pill container, you can open one compartment at a time, avoiding potential spills of beads from neighboring compartments.
- **Fishing Tackle Box.** Store fly-fishing hooks, weights, and flies in a pill container.
- **Screw Storage.** A pill container stores a nice selection of small screws, nuts, and washers.
- **Seed Storage.** Fill each compartment with seeds for rosemary, carrots, dill, or tomatoes—plants for which you need only a few seeds at a time.
- **Travel Spice Rack.** Fill each compartment of a pill container with a different spice for camping. Place a label on the lid of each compartment to identify each spice.

How to Vacuum Pack with a Vacuum Cleaner

WHAT YOU NEED

- Plastic kitchen trash bags
- Vacuum cleaner with hose attachment
- Hair band (or rubber band)

WHAT TO DO

1. Place bulky clothes, blankets, or even a foam mattress pad inside a plastic kitchen trash bag.
2. Remove any cleaning attachment from the vacuum cleaner hose, insert the end of the hose through a hair band (or doubled-over rubber band), and slide the tie one foot up the hose.
3. With your hand, bunch up the mouth of the plastic trash bag and hold it closed lightly.
4. Insert the end of the vacuum cleaner hose into the top opening in the trash bag (pressed against an item inside, not the plastic side of the bag), and gather the mouth of the bag shut around the hose.
5. Slide the hair band (or rubber band) down the tube and over the bunched-up mouth of the bag to hold it in place and form a seal.
6. Turn on the vacuum cleaner and suck the air from the plastic trash bag until it stops shrinking.
7. Slide the tube out from the bag with the vacuum cleaner still running, and holding the bunched-up section of the bag, spin the bag to tighten it shut.
8. Use the hair band to seal the bag shut.
9. Turn off the vacuum cleaner.

HOW IT WORKS

The vacuum cleaner sucks the excess air from the bag, creating a vacuum seal and compressing the contents inside.

Rather than using kitchen trash bags (which are 0.95 mil), you can use thicker trash bags (1.05 mil) or contractor-grade trash bags (3.0 mil) so the bags don't accidentally rip open as easily.

How to Deodorize a Suitcase with Dryer Sheets

WHAT YOU NEED
- Dryer sheets

WHAT TO DO
1. Place the smelly suitcase, trunk, or duffle bag open outside on a porch to air out for several hours.
2. Place several dryer sheets inside the suitcase.
3. Seal the suitcase shut and let it stand undisturbed for one week.
4. When packing the suitcase, place a few dryer sheets between clothing items in your suitcase.

HOW IT WORKS
Dryer sheets keep your clothes smelling fresh and prevent them from absorbing any mustiness from old luggage.

IN THE BAG
When storing suitcases, leave the zippers open so the luggage can air out. Here are a few more tips to keep your luggage fresh:

- **Baking Soda.** Place a bowl filled with baking soda inside the suitcase and close the suitcase. Let it stand undisturbed for several days, then remove the bowl of baking soda. Baking soda chemically neutralizes odors by turning into a sodium salt and giving off water and carbon dioxide.
- **Garbage Bags.** Before packing dirty laundry in a suitcase, place the soiled clothes in a plastic garbage bag and seal it shut.
- **Kitty Litter.** Place unused kitty litter inside the suitcase to absorb the odors and close the suitcase. Let it stand undisturbed for several days and then remove the kitty litter. The pure, refined clay absorbs odors and moisture, which prevents and reduces mold and mildew.
- **Newspaper.** To deodorize musty luggage, fill a suitcase or trunk with crumpled pages of newspaper, close it, and let it sit for two weeks. The newsprint absorbs foul odors.
- **Soap.** To keep luggage smelling fresh, tuck a wrapped bar of soap inside a suitcase before storing it. When you take out the suitcase to go traveling, leave the bar of soap inside to keep your clothes smelling fresh.

How to Fix a Broken Luggage Wheel with Duct Tape

WHAT YOU NEED

- Duct tape
- Utility knife
- Black electrical tape (optional)

WHAT TO DO

1. If the rubber wheel on a suitcase cracks and falls off, leaving behind an inner metal roller, tear a strip of duct tape the width of the wheel.
2. Wrap the strip of duct tape tightly around the inner metal roller (making certain the width of the tape is centered on the roller) in the direction the wheel turns (from front to back) so the tape does not unravel when you roll the suitcase.
3. Continue wrapping strips of duct tape around the wheel until the layers of duct tape attain the same diameter as the opposite wheel.
4. If necessary, use a utility knife to carefully trim or bevel the sides of the duct tape tire to prevent the sides from rubbing against the frame of the suitcase.
5. If desired, cover the finished wheel with a strip of black electrical tape to cover the adhesive on the beveled edge and give the improvised tire the same color as the opposite tire.

HOW IT WORKS

The duct tape creates enough thickness to temporarily double as a spare tire for the luggage.

WATCHING THE WHEELS

You can also replace a broken luggage wheel with a Rollerblade wheel, provided you have one of matching size. Remove your broken luggage wheel with a screwdriver or hex wrench, reusing any existing washers. If the wheel is attached with rivets, you need to replace the entire bolt and axle. An inline skate wheel will actually be more durable and roll smoother than a standard luggage wheel. Adding a colorful Rollerblade wheel to your luggage will also make your bag easier to identify at baggage claim.

How to Identify Luggage with Nail Polish

WHAT YOU NEED
- A brightly colored nail polish
- Suitcase

WHAT TO DO
1. Carefully paint the heads of any screws on your suitcase (generally found on both sides of the handles) with a coat of brightly colored nail polish.
2. Let it dry.
3. Repeat if necessary, to give the nail polish a second coat.

HOW IT WORKS
When your suitcase comes through the baggage claim at your destination, you'll immediately spot the unique spots of color on your luggage. Unlike a colored tag or ribbon tied through the luggage strap, the brightly colored screws are not easily removed.

A WHOLE BAG OF TRICKS
Buying a uniquely colored suitcase with an outlandish design reduces the chances that other travelers on your flight, train, or bus will have the same luggage as you, minimizing the likelihood that others will accidentally mistake your luggage for their own. Here are more ways to make your luggage easily identifiable:
- **Colorful Luggage Tags.** Attach one or more unique and sturdy luggage tags to the handle of your suitcase so you can easily recognize the tag and bag from a distance.
- **Duct Tape.** Tape brightly colored or pattered duct tape to the luggage in the shape of your initial or any design of your choosing.
- **Electrical Tape.** Apply a few strips of colorful electrical tape to your luggage to make an eye-catching bag.
- **Fabric Paint.** Use fabric paint in glitter colors to paint wild designs on your fabric bags.
- **Garbage Bag.** Place your suitcase inside a large plastic black garbage bag and use masking tape to write your initial on the outside of the

bag. Your luggage will be easily recognizable and simultaneously protected from rain.

- **Luggage Straps.** Buy colorful luggage straps to wrap around your checked bags.
- **Ribbon or Yarn.** Adorn you luggage by tying a piece of brightly colored ribbon or strips of yarn braided together to the handle of your luggage.
- **Sponge or Scrubber.** Attach a loofah sponge on a rope or a colorful nylon body scrubber on a rope to your luggage.

OFF THE BEATEN TRACK

How to Weigh Your Luggage

To avoid being slapped with additional fees at the airport, weigh your bags in advance to make sure they do not exceed the weight restrictions.

- Check with your airline to confirm weight restrictions for your luggage. Understand that your class of travel and your destination determine how much luggage you can bring.
- With your bag fully packed, place the bag on a bathroom scale. If the bag does not fit on the scale, weigh yourself on the scale and record your weight. Lift your luggage, step on the scale, and record the combined weight of you and the bag. Subtract the first number from the second number to calculate the weight of the bag.
- If a scale is unavailable, consider bringing your luggage to a gym.
- Purchase an inexpensive handheld luggage scale. The scale clips onto the handle of your bag, and you then lift the scale with the bag attached to determine the weight. You can also pack the lightweight scale into your bag, so you're always prepared for this scenario.
- If your bag exceeds the weight limit, place some of the heavier items in your carry-on bag. Airlines restrict the dimensions of your carry-on bag, but they rarely check the weight.

How to Prevent Toiletries from Exploding with Plastic Wrap

WHAT YOU NEED
- Scissors
- Plastic wrap
- Masking tape (optional)
- Ziplock freezer bags

WHAT TO DO
1. To prevent bottles and tubes of liquid products like shampoo and conditioner from exploding and making a mess inside your suitcase, use a pair of scissors to cut a 2-inch square of plastic wrap.
2. Remove the cap from the bottle, jar, or tube, set the plastic square on top of the mouth, and replace the cap securely.
3. For added security with a flip cap, tape down the flip cap with masking tape and then adhere another strip of tape around the circumference.
4. Place the bottle or tube in a freezer bag, zip the bag shut most of the way (leaving an opening roughly 1 inch long), suck the remaining air from the bag, and seal the bag shut.

5. Wrap the excess plastic from the bag around the bottle or tube.
6. Nestle the bottle or tube in the center of your suitcase, surrounded by clothes or tucked inside a shoe or sneaker for additional protection.

HOW IT WORKS
The plastic wrap seals the opening in the tube or bottle shut, so if the cap accidentally flips open or the bottle gets squeezed, no liquid will burst out. The masking tape prevents flip caps from accidentally flipping open.

SPILLING THE BEANS

Here are a few other items you can use to pack your toiletry items safely for travel:

- **Binder Clip.** If your razor has no protective cap, attach a large binder clip over the blades to avoid cutting your fingers by accident when reaching into your toiletry or makeup bag.

- **Contact Lens Case.** Rather than packing bottles and jars of makeup that might accidentally spill, pour some of the cream or lotion into a clean, empty contact lens case.

- **Plastic Prescription Bottle.** Store cotton swabs in a plastic prescription bottle to keep them dry and organized.

- **Tic Tac Box.** An empty Tic Tac box makes an excellent container for storing bobby pins.

EVERY TRICK IN THE BOOK
In a Bind

Here are a few additional ways to use binder clips:

- **Beer Stacker.** To store cans or bottles of beer on their sides, stacked in a pyramid in a mini-fridge with wire shelves, attach a binder clip to one of the metal wires to create a bookend.

- **Belt Holder.** Use a binder clip to hold the long end of a belt to the rest of the belt, to prevent it from flapping.

- **Cable Tie.** Declutter all those cables and wires under your desk by clipping them together with binder clips.

- **Clothespin Substitute.** Need to attach a wet garment to a clothesline? In a pinch, binder clips work beautifully.

- **Money Clip.** Fold your bills in half and hold them together with a binder clip.

- **Toothpaste Squeezer.** Attach a binder clip to the end of toothpaste tube to hold the rolled-up end in place.

How to Lock a Suitcase with a Paper Clip

WHAT YOU NEED

- Paper clip (or metal key ring)

WHAT TO DO

1. Zipper the suitcase securely shut so that the eyeholes of the zipper keys line up.
2. Insert the end of the paper clip into the aligned eyeholes, and rotate the metal clip until it is firmly attached.

HOW IT WORKS

The paper clip holds the two zipper keys together so the zipper cannot be accidentally opened. While this technique may not stop a thief from breaking into your bag, it does create an obstruction that will certainly slow and possibly dissuade a thief seeking an easy heist.

EVERY TRICK IN THE BOOK
A Familiar Ring

If you have an abundance of key rings in a variety of sizes, you can use them for much more than simply holding keys.

- **Closet Space Savers.** Slip a key ring over the neck of a hanger, and hook a second hanger on the ring.
- **Measuring Spoon Connector.** Use a key ring to attach your measuring spoons together.
- **Napkin Rings.** Use large key rings with decorative attachments as festive or themed napkin rings.
- **Potted Plant or Hummingbird Feeder Hangers.** Attach a number of key rings together to create a chain for hanging potted plants or hummingbird feeders.
- **Wind Chime Hangers.** Hook a number of key rings together to create a chain to hang a wind chime.
- **Zipper Key Replacement.** If the key on a zipper breaks off, attach a key ring through the hole in the slider and, if desired, add a decorative toggle to the key ring.

How to Hide Money in a Pair of Blue Jeans

WHAT YOU NEED
- Scissors
- Money
- Blue jeans

WHAT TO DO
1. Hold the pair of jeans to find the inner hem behind the zipper.
2. Using scissors, carefully cut a horizontal opening approximately 1 inch long along the top of the inner hem.
3. Roll up the money and slide it through the opening, and push the roll of bills down toward the bottom of the newly created pocket.
4. Don the jeans.
5. To remove the roll of money from the hidden pocket, simply press your fingers at the bottom of the pocket to push the roll upward toward the opening.

HOW IT WORKS
The hem behind the zipper in a pair of blue jeans forms a slender vertical pocket that can be accessed by cutting a horizontal slit in the top of the hem. A slender roll of money inserted in the pocket remains hidden inside the jeans. (Note that an airport full-body scanner will detect the roll of money.)

STASH YOUR CASH
- You can also hide your money in a long-sleeve shirt. While wearing a long-sleeve shirt, fold back one of the cuffs of one sleeve, slip your money inside the cuff, and then continue folding up the sleeve past your elbow. Roll up the opposite sleeve to match.

- The cushioning pad inside every shoe and sneaker creates a secret compartment. Remove the pad, slip money into the footwear, and reinsert the pad.
- Retailers sell a watertight container that looks like an ordinary SPF-25 sunscreen bottle that can hold your cash, credit cards, keys, and cell phone.
- When you're at the beach, place your cell phone, wallet, and keys inside a disposable diaper, roll it up, and fasten the adhesive tabs. Leave the diaper on your beach towel (provided you have young children to complete the charade).

How to Hide Money in a Necktie

WHAT YOU NEED

- Necktie
- Stitch-remover tool
- Needle
- Thread
- Piece of fabric, 3 inches long by 2½ inches wide
- Velcro strip, 5 inches long

WHAT TO DO

1. Most ties have a stitch sewn up the center of the back of the tie to hold together the two sides of decorative fabric. Using the stitch-remover tool, remove the stitches from the bottom 5 inches of the wide end of the back of the tie.

2. Most ties contain a stiff fabric core to maintain the shape of the tie. Sew the piece of fabric to the inner fabric core (but not through the front side of the decorative fabric) to create a pocket.

3. Sew the opposing sides of the Velcro strip to the opposite fabric flaps of the backside of the tie.

4. Insert your folded cash or credit cards in the pocket, close the flaps of the back of the tie, sealing the Velcro strips securely, and wear the tie as usual.

HOW IT WORKS

The Velcro strips keep the back of the tie sealed shut, concealing the secret pocket containing your cash and credit cards.

How to Assemble an Emergency Kit in a Prescription Pill Bottle

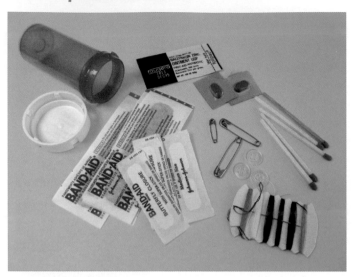

WHAT YOU NEED

- Clean, empty plastic prescription pill bottle, label removed

For an Automotive Kit

- Coins for parking meters

For an Emergency Kit

- Batteries (AA)
- Bouillon cubes
- Miniature flashlight
- Tea and coffee pouches
- Twist ties

For a Fishing Kit

- Fishing line
- Hooks
- Weights
- Lures
- Bobber

For a First Aid Kit

- Adhesive bandages
- Aspirin or other nonsteroidal anti-inflammatory drugs (NSAID)
- Alcohol swabs
- Small tube or packet of antibiotic ointment
- Gauze pads

For a Key Kit
- Duplicate keys to the house, car, or strongbox

For a Sewing Kit
- 2 sewing needles
- Pins
- Thread (various colors wrapped around a toothpick)
- Shirt buttons
- Safety pins

WHAT TO DO
1. Fill the plastic prescription pill bottle with any combination of the aforementioned items to make a compact emergency kit.
2. Secure the lid shut.

HOW IT WORKS
An emergency kit stored in a plastic prescription pill bottle remains watertight and conveniently sized to easily fit in your bags.

SPIN THE BOTTLE
You can also use a prescription pill bottle to carry any of the following:
- **Batteries.** Use pill bottles to organize batteries.
- **Bobby Pins and Hair Clips.** These hair accessories can be easily stored and organized in pill bottles.
- **Craft Items.** Store beads, cake-piping tips, and needles.
- **Matches.** Store wooden matches in a clean, empty, plastic prescription pill bottle. The waterproof canister keeps the matches secure and dry. If you're storing wooden matches, be sure to remove a striker from a matchbook or matchbox and slip it inside the canister as well. Even if you're stashing strike-anywhere matches in the canister, a striker stored in a waterproof canister may come in handy if you're soaking wet or stranded in a drenched area. You can also include a few cotton balls, which can be pulled apart to create tinder.
- **Keys.** Hide a key inside a prescription pill bottle and then bury the canister in the backyard and cover the spot with a marker, like a rock.
- **Seeds.** Store seeds in prescription pill bottles to keep them dry and easily accessible.
- **Spices, Herbs, and Condiments.** A prescription pill bottle makes a water-resistant container for salt, pepper, oregano, and teas.

How to Prevent Necklaces from Tangling with a Drinking Straw

WHAT YOU NEED

- Scissors
- Plastic drinking straws
- Plastic wrap

WHAT TO DO

1. Cut a straw the length of one-half the length of your delicate chain jewelry.
2. Feed the end of the chain through two straws and clasp the necklace closed.
3. Place the necklaces between two sheets of plastic wrap.

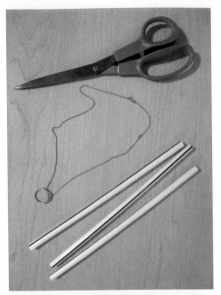

HOW IT WORKS

The plastic straws prevent the delicate chain from knotting and tangling, and the plastic wrap prevents the necklace from jangling inside your suitcase.

DON'T GET YOURSELF TIED UP IN KNOTS

To disentangle a knot from a fine chain necklace, place the chain on a sheet of paper and sprinkle some baby powder or cornstarch on the knot. Using two sewing pins or needles, slowly and carefully pick out the knot. The baby powder or cornstarch lubricates the metal, making the knots easier to remove.

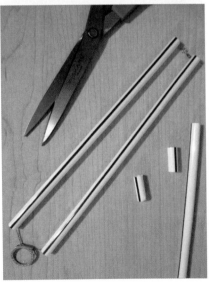

How to Protect a Wine Bottle with Sneakers

WHAT YOU NEED

- Ziplock freezer bag, 2-gallon
- Sock
- Pair of sneakers with ample padding

WHAT TO DO

1. Place the unopened wine bottle in the freezer bag and zip the bag shut most of the way, leaving an opening roughly 1 inch long. Suck the remaining air from the bag and seal the bag shut.

2. Wrap the excess plastic from the bag around the wine bottle.

3. Slide the wine bottle inside the sock.

4. Loosen the laces of the sneakers to make ample room for the wine bottle.

5. Insert the base of the bottle in one sneaker, wedging it tightly.

6. Place the neck of the bottle into the other sneaker all the way up to the toe.

7. Nestle the sneaker-encased wine bottle in the center of your suitcase, surrounded by clothes for additional padding to prevent shifting.

8. If you don't have a pair of sneakers, wrap the wine bottle in a sweater or a pair of jeans.

HOW IT WORKS

The padded sneakers provide sufficient cushioning to protect the glass bottle and minimize the vibrations that can negatively affect wine. The ziplock bag provides additional protection should the bottle break and leak.

How to Make a Pair of Slippers from Maxi Pads

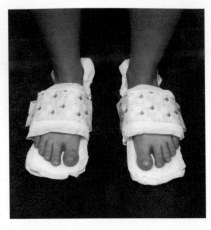

WHAT YOU NEED

- 6 maxi pads
- Confetti or a decorative strip of paper

WHAT TO DO

1. Place one maxi pad (adhesive strip up) on a flat surface and peel off the paper protecting the adhesive strip.
2. Peel off the paper protecting the adhesive strip from a second maxi pad, wrap the maxi pad (adhesive side out) around the middle of your foot, and adhere the ends to each other to make a loose loop.
3. Place one flat side of the loop on the exposed adhesive strip of the first maxi pad to create a strap for your foot.
4. Peel off the paper protecting the adhesive strip from the third maxi pad.
5. Thread the third maxi pad (adhesive side down) through the loop and line it up to cover the first maxi pad (adhesive side up).
6. Press the third maxi pad firmly in place to attach it to the first maxi pad.
7. Repeat steps 1 through 6 with the remaining three maxi pads.
8. Adhere confetti or a decorative strip of paper to the exposed adhesive strips on the two loops that serve as the straps.
9. Slip your feet into the loops.

HOW IT WORKS

The adhesive strips hold the maxi pads together, and the resulting slippers are comfortably padded and surprisingly cozy.

EVERY TRICK IN THE BOOK
How to Maximize a Maxi Pad

- **Clean a Car or Truck Windshield.** Peel the adhesive strip from the back of a maxi pad, adhere the pad to the palm of your hand, and use it to wipe down the windshield.
- **Prevent Perspiration Stains on the Inside of a Hat Headband.** Peel off the adhesive strip on the back of a maxi pad, and stick the maxi pad inside your hat along the headband that rests against your forehead. The maxi pad will absorb perspiration. Replace the maxi pad when necessary.
- **Protect a Blister or Corn.** Using a pair of scissors, cut a maxi pad into a donut shape, and place it over the blister, leaving the hole over the blister and letting the adhesive strip adhere to the skin. The maxi pad will protect the blister while it heals.
- **Clean Eyeglasses.** In a pinch, you can wipe the lenses of a pair of eyeglasses clean with a maxi pad.
- **Give Yourself a Sponge Bath.** If you don't have time to take a bath, saturate a maxi pad with water and use it as a washcloth to give yourself a sponge bath.
- **Improvise Nursing Pads when Breastfeeding.** A maxi pad makes an excellent substitute for nursing pads. Cut two circles from the panty liner, and use the adhesive strip to adhere the absorbent pads inside the bra cups.
- **Apply or Remove Makeup.** In a pinch a maxi pad makes an excellent makeup sponge for applying or removing makeup.
- **Bring Down a Fever.** If you don't have a washcloth, saturate a maxi pad with cold water and place it over your forehead to bring down a fever.
- **Prevent Blisters on Your Feet.** Use a pair of scissors to cut a pair of ultra-thin maxi pads to make shoe insert pads, to prevent your ankles and heels from rubbing against the top edges of the shoes. The ultra-thin maxi pads are the perfect thickness and are also available with deodorant to prevent smelly feet.
- **Protect Your Knees when Scrubbing Floors.** Peel the adhesive strips from two maxi pads and stick the pads to your knees for cushioned support.
- **Prevent Perspiration Stains on Shirts, Blouses, or Jackets.** Peel off the adhesive strip on the back of a maxi pad, and stick the maxi pad inside the armpit of a dress shirt, blouse, or jacket to absorb excess perspiration.
- **Shine Shoes.** After applying polish to shoes, buff with maxi pads.

How to Waterproof a Map with Hairspray

WHAT YOU NEED
- Newspaper
- Rubber gloves
- Safety goggles
- Dust mask (or bandana)
- A can of aerosol hairspray
- Ziplock freezer bag

WHAT TO DO
1. Spread the newspaper on a working surface outdoors or in a well-ventilated area.
2. Open the map, and place it on top of the newspaper.
3. Wearing the rubber gloves, safety goggles, and dusk mask, spray a light coat of hairspray over the surface of the map.
4. Let the surface dry for 30 minutes.
5. Flip the map over, and again wearing the rubber gloves, safety goggles, and dusk mask, spray a thin coat of hairspray over the back of the map.
6. Let the surface dry for 30 minutes.
7. Repeat the entire procedure to give both sides of the map a second coat of hairspray.
8. Fold up the map and pack it inside a ziplock bag.

HOW IT WORKS
The fixative in the hairspray gives the map a waterproof coating, and the ziplock bag further protects the map from moisture and abrasion.

MAP IT OUT
Many companies now produce waterproof maps, but if you need other ways to protect an existing paper map, try:
- **Clear Packaging Tape.** Cover both sides of the map with strips of clear packaging tape until you have laminated the entire map.
- **Con-Tact Paper.** Cover both sides of a map with clear Con-Tact paper to create a waterproof seal, and then trim the edges with a pair of scissors or a utility knife. Trace your route with a dry erase marker, which you can wipe off after the trip.

How to Open a Locked Suitcase with a Ballpoint Pen

WHAT YOU NEED
- Ballpoint pen

WHAT TO DO
1. To get into a locked zippered suitcase, jab the point of a ballpoint pen into the sealed zipper combs near the lock— puncturing the seal made by the zipper teeth.
2. With the pen inserted into the perforation between the zipper teeth, glide the pen along the zipper to open the suitcase.
3. To reseal the suitcase, simply grab the lock holding the zipper mechanism shut and zip up the suitcase.
4. Return the zipper mechanism to its original position, leaving no sign that anyone has tampered with the suitcase.

HOW IT WORKS
The zipper is a meshed-tooth slider fastener, and jabbing and sliding a sharp object between the fastened meshed teeth separates them, just like the mechanical slider does.

LEFT HOLDING THE BAG
- In 1922, the B. F. Goodrich Company gave the trademark name Zipper to its new rubber galoshes with new "hookless fasteners." Goodrich reportedly coined the word "zipper," onomatopoeia for the sound the device made when he zipped up his boots. The catchy name made the zipper a household word and common fastener on clothing.
- In 1935, fashion designer Elsa Schiaparelli introduced a line of clothing bursting with decorative colored zippers of various sizes, turning the zipper into a popular fashion statement.
- It was also in 1935 that Hungarian newspaper editor Ladislas Biro, frustrated with the ink pens he used at work, teamed up with his brother George to develop the ballpoint pen. Their new design included a rolling ball at the tip and the quick-drying ink used to print newspapers.

How to Live out of Grocery Tote Bags

WHAT YOU NEED

- Several reusable canvas grocery tote bags (one for each night of your road trip)

WHAT TO DO

1. Rather than lugging a heavy suitcase into a new hotel each night, pack individual canvas grocery tote bags with one day's worth of clothes—a shirt, a pair of pants, a pair of socks, and underwear.
2. Place your toiletry kit in the first canvas bag.
3. Place all the packed tote bags in the trunk of your car.
4. When you check in to your hotel, bring the first canvas tote (including the toiletry kit).
5. In the morning, place your dirty clothes in the tote, place it back in the trunk, and move the toiletry kit to your second canvas tote bag.

HOW IT WORKS

You still travel with a sufficient amount of clothes, but each night you reach into the trunk and grab one small canvas tote bag containing a change of clothes and your toiletry kit—eliminating the hassle of hauling a large suitcase into a new hotel room each night.

LIVING OUT OF A SUITCASE

To keep reusable grocery tote bags organized in your trunk, simply place a plastic bin in your trunk and fill it with the totes.

2

AIRPLANES AND AIRPORTS

You show up to the airport to catch the red-eye, only to discover that the plane won't start boarding for another three hours. How do you catch some shut-eye? When you finally board the plane, it's filled with screaming babies, and your're crammed in the middle seat, sandwiched between two flatulent fatties. How do you sleep now?

How to Sleep Comfortably in an Airport with a Newspaper

WHAT YOU NEED

- Newspaper

WHAT TO DO

1. Find an inconspicuous corner of the airport waiting area, ideally against a wall and behind a row of seats.
2. Place the newspaper on the floor, spreading out the sheets to cover an area the length of your body.
3. Lie down on the sheets of newspaper.
4. Place a section of newspaper over your face to form a tent.

HOW IT WORKS

The newspaper insulates your body from any germs on the carpeted floor, and the tent of newspaper over your face creates darkness and a sense of privacy.

You can fashion a pillow from a sweatshirt or sweater (folded to the size of a pillow) or a down jacket (folded to the thickness of a pillow). A down jacket also doubles as a makeshift blanket.

SLEEP ON IT

- The website www.sleepinginairports.net offers tips for sleeping comfortably and safely in airports and rates airports based on "sleepability."
- Actress Yennis Cheung, who played the casino cashier in the 2012 James Bond film *Skyfall*, told the *Express* that when her family first moved to Hong Kong when she was a few months old, they slept on newspaper.
- In "Putting Myself Together" in the *New Yorker*, Antiguan American novelist Jamaica Kincaid recalls her poverty-stricken early life and tells of giving herself coffee enemas and sleeping on newspaper.

OFF THE BEATEN TRACK

Get Access to First-Class Airport Lounges

Instead of waiting around a crowded airport terminal with screaming babies, smelly restrooms, and nothing to eat but overpriced
burgers at T.G.I. Friday's, imagine yourself relaxing in a spacious
executive lounge with a complimentary bar (fully stocked), a
glorious buffet, comfortable leather chairs, free Wi-Fi, big-screen
televisions, complimentary computers with Internet access,
complimentary headphones for your music-listening pleasure,
complimentary magazines and newspapers, and spa-like showers
and changing rooms so you can freshen up in style. If you've got a
tediously long layover, your flight has been delayed endlessly, or
you have to check out of your hotel with nowhere else to go, an
executive airport lounge provides a remarkable oasis of peace.
But how do you get inside these fortresses of solitude if you're
not traveling first-class?

- **Buy a Day Pass Online.** If you buy yourself lunch or dinner in an
airport, you'll wind up spending roughly $20 for a Styrofoam bowl
of kung pao chicken and a can of lukewarm Miller Lite served in an
overcrowded food court teeming with wheeled luggage. But if you
buy yourself day access to an executive lounge (ranging in price
from $29 to $50), you can enjoy an upscale all-you-can-eat buffet

and ply yourself with all the Chivas Regal you can drink. Rather than paying the full price, go online before you arrive at the airport and buy the pass for up to 50 percent off the regular price. Poof! You're in the lap of luxury for the additional cost of a supersized Big Mac value meal.

- **Buy an Annual Pass.** If you fly the same airline constantly, consider buying an annual pass to the airline lounge. Instead of paying cash for the exorbitant $450–$500 annual fee, buy the pass with frequent flyer miles. Or try to get your employer to pay for it. (By the way, the annual pass allows you to bring at least one guest for free—cutting your cost in half and giving you a great way to impress business associates, appease a spouse, or seduce a hot prospect traveling coach.)

- **Get Ballsy.** As mentioned above, annual pass holders are entitled to bring a guest for free. Stand by the door to the first-class lounge and ask someone about to step inside to take you in as a guest (offering to pay the guest fee, if there is one). You can be completely up front or tell 'em, "Drat! My annual pass just expired last week!"

- **Buy a Low-Cost Universal Club Pass.** If you plan to fly on a variety of airlines over the next year, you can buy an annual pass that gives you access to the first-class lounges for a wide range of airlines. For $99 Priority Pass gives you access to more than 600 airline lounges in more than 100 countries and more than 300 cities worldwide (provided you pay an additional $27 for each club visit). Plus, you can bring a guest (for yet another $27).

- **Upgrade to Business Class on an International Flight Using Frequent Flyer Miles.** If you've got frequent flyer miles, upgrading to business class usually gets you use of the lounge. It costs a ton of miles, but if you're determined to pamper yourself with both a business-class seat and a relaxing wait in the first-class lounge, this little trick opens the door to the Cave of Wonders.

- **Apply for a Kick-Ass Credit Card.** If you're willing to pay the pricey annual fee, some fancy-schmancy credit cards give you and your immediate family access to specific airlines' first-class lounges—provided you have a ticket to fly that day on that particular airline. Hoity-toity credit cards that provide this service include the American Express Platinum Card ($450 annual fee) and the Ameriprise World Elite MasterCard ($150 annual fee). The hefty price tag does include a host of other intriguing benefits—like

extended warranties, concierge services, and bragging rights—
that may make the steep cost worthwhile to you.

- **Hunt for Fly-by-Night Bargains.** It sounds incongruous, but
the airlines actually put annual memberships and day passes to
their first-class lounges on sale (for short bursts of time)—with
savings of up to 43 percent off the regular price. Unfortunately,
the best way to learn about these discounts is by signing yourself
up to receive spam from the airlines that interest you most. For
instance, you'll have to register for Delta's email blast, "Like" the
airline on Facebook, and follow Delta on Twitter. But your fanatical
devotion can pay off big-time.

- **Get a Frequent Flyer
Discount.** If you've got
gazillions of frequent
flyer miles in one
particular airline's
program, and if that
airline has knighted you
with some type of crème
de la crème status,
you may be eligible
for a discount (typically 20 percent) off the annual membership
to the first-class lounge, or a free subscription to the in-flight
magazine—your choice.

- **Check Out eBay and Craigslist.** You can sometimes find
someone attempting to sell an airport lounge day pass dirt cheap
on a resale website. Before buying a pass from an unknown seller,
verify that the terms and conditions printed on the pass state
that the pass is transferable to someone not related to the buyer.
Confirm the expiration date, and think twice before buying a day
pass for lounges operated by Pan Am, TWA, or Eastern.

- **Do a Little Homework.** Before you slap down your money to use
any airport lounge, make sure the facility provides the amenities
you desire. Otherwise, you may be paying for the privilege of sitting
in a storage closet that makes the terminal waiting area look like
Barbie's Malibu Dreamhouse. Consult the reviews at AirlineQuality.
com and LoungeGuide.net, or ask for a tour of the lounge before
you say "I do."

How to Incapacitate a Hijacker with a Pot of Coffee

WHAT YOU NEED
- Pot of boiling-hot coffee from the kitchen area of the plane

WHAT TO DO
1. Carefully grab a pot of boiling-hot coffee from one of the food trolleys or the galley.
2. Hurl the hot coffee in the hijacker's face (or trip the hijacker and then pour hot coffee in his face).
3. Whack the incapacitated hijacker in the head with the coffee pot.

HOW IT WORKS
The hot coffee burns the hijacker, diverting his attention long enough for other passengers to help subdue him.

WAKE UP AND SMELL THE COFFEE
Things aboard an airplane that can be used as a weapon to confront a hijacker:
- **Crash Ax.** This tool, stored in the cockpit for the purpose of hacking through the skin of an airplane in an emergency, can be used like a regular ax.
- **Fire Extinguisher.** Discharge the halon fire extinguisher to temporarily incapacitate the hijacker and then hit him in the head with the butt of the heavy metal canister.
- **Nosedive.** The pilot swoops into a nosedive, creating zero-g forces that pin the hijacker to the airplane's ceiling.

COFFEE, TEA, OR ME
On February 7, 2002, Pablo Moreira Mosca, a 29-year-old bank employee from Uruguay, attempted to break into the cockpit of United Airlines Flight 855 from Miami to Buenos Aires. Mosca crashed into the reinforced cockpit door and maneuvered his upper body into the cockpit, before the copilot hit him with the blunt end of an ax. Fellow passengers helped subdue him and tie him to a seat using their seat belts.

How to Relieve an Air-Pressure Earache with a Drinking Cup

WHAT YOU NEED
- Tissue or paper towel
- Plastic or paper cup

WHAT TO DO
1. Carefully dampen a tissue or a paper towel with hot water (hot tea or hot coffee will also work), ball it up, and place it in the bottom of a plastic or paper cup.
2. Hold the cup over your affected ear.

HOW IT WORKS
The steam from the hot water softens the wax in your ear, alleviating the pain caused by the change in pressure in an airplane.

GETTING AN EARFUL
- Flying in an airplane while suffering from ear problems can result in excruciating pain. Taking an over-the-counter decongestant an hour before the flight can relieve the congestion in the eustachian tube, preventing pain during changes in air pressure.
- The mere act of swallowing, yawning, chewing gum, or drinking a glass of water opens the eustachian tubes, allowing them to drain.
- In 1935, during an exhibition of Van Gogh's paintings at New York's Museum of Modern Art, prankster Hugh Troy hung on the wall a velvet-lined shadowbox containing a piece of dried beef he had carved into the shape of an ear, with a sign that read, "This is the ear that Van Gogh cut off and sent to his mistress Dec. 24, 1888."
- In the 1966 movie *Fantastic Voyage*, starring Raquel Welch, the shrunken scientists traveling through a sedated human body in a microscopic submarine pass through the inner ear. When a nurse in the outside surgery room accidentally drops a tool, the resulting sound, amplified by the eardrum, causes the ship to toss and turn uncontrollably.

EVERY TRICK IN THE BOOK

All Ears

- **Chewing Gum.** Alleviate an earache caused by the change in pressure in an airplane by chewing a piece of gum. The muscular action of chewing gum opens the eustachian tubes, which run from the back of the throat to the middle ear.
- **Hard Candy.** Relieve an earache caused by the change in pressure in an airplane by sucking on a piece of hard candy. The candy causes your mouth to salivate, and the resulting swallowing action opens the eustachian tubes in your ears.
- **Vodka.** If bacteria is causing the pain your ear, and you don't have rubbing alcohol (because you're flying aboard an airplane), pour some vodka (available in a mini-bottle from the flight attendants) into the affected ear and let it drain out. The alcohol in the vodka kills the bacteria. If you prefer to use an ear dropper, insert the end of a plastic drinking straw or a hollow swizzle stick into the vodka, cover the open end of the straw with your finger, hold the straw over your ear, and release your finger from the straw.
- **Ziplock Freezer Bag.** Fill a ziplock bag with warm water, seal securely, and hold the bag against your ear as a hot compress. The warm bag conforms to the contours of your ear and provides relief.

How to Make Noise-Canceling Headphones with a Tennis Ball

WHAT YOU NEED
- Utility knife or scissors
- Tennis ball
- Pair of panty hose

WHAT TO DO

1. Before leaving for the airport, use a utility knife or scissors to carefully cut the tennis ball in half. Do not bring the knife or scissors to the airport.
2. On the flight, place the pair of panty hose over your head, wearing the waistband like a headband.
3. Insert each tennis ball under the panty hose and over each one of your ears.
4. Adjust the waistband to hold the tennis balls securely in place.

HOW IT WORKS

The pair of panty hose holds the tennis ball halves in place over your ears, the spherical shell (a 6-milimeter-thick composite of rubber and cloth) significantly muffles the surrounding noise, and the resulting appearance makes an interesting fashion statement.

OFF THE BEATEN TRACK
How to Check Your Carry-On Bag for Free

If you wait to board the plane last, you can easily volunteer to check your luggage in the cargo hold, which the flight attendants will do for free.

EVERY TRICK IN THE BOOK

Tennis Anyone?

Here are a few more ways you can share the love with tennis balls:

- **Store Valuables.** Make a 2-inch slit along one seam of a tennis ball, then place valuables inside. If you hide the doctored tennis ball among your other sports equipment, remember not to use it.
- **Fluff Your Down Jacket in the Dryer and Reduce Static Cling.** Throw in a handful of tennis balls to fluff the down while the jacket is tumbling in the dryer.
- **Childproof the Sharp Corners of Furniture.** Cut old tennis balls in half or quarters and use packaging tape to tape the sections over sharp corners of coffee tables, end tables, cabinets, dining room tables, and other pieces of furniture that might be dangerous to a small child.
- **Make a Walker Glide Easily.** Cut a hole in two tennis balls and fit them on the back feet of the walker.
- **Remove Cobwebs from Unreachable Places.** Wrap a tennis ball inside a dust cloth secured with a few rubber bands, then toss at the distant cobweb.
- **Strengthen Your Grip and Relieve Stress.** Squeeze a tennis ball in each hand.
- **Prevent Snoring.** Sew a tennis ball inside a pocket on the back of your pajama top to prevent you from sleeping on your back.
- **Stop a Deck Chair from Slipping Through the Cracks of a Dock.** Slit four tennis balls and fit them on the feet of the deck chair.

How to Fashion a Sleep Mask from Maxi Pads

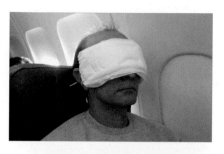

WHAT YOU NEED

- 2 maxi pads
- 2 shoelaces

WHAT TO DO

1. Place one maxi pad (adhesive strip up) on a flat surface and peel off the paper protecting the adhesive strip.

2. Locate the midpoint of the first shoelace, and then carefully place the midsection of the shoelace lengthwise along the adhesive strip on the maxi pad.

3. Locate the midpoint of the second shoelace, then carefully place the midsection of the second shoelace lengthwise (¼ inch below the first shoelace) along the adhesive strip on the maxi pad.

4. Peel off the paper protecting the adhesive strip from the second maxi pad.

5. Line up the second maxi pad (adhesive side down) to cover the first maxi pad (adhesive side up) and the attached sections of the shoelaces.

6. Press the second maxi pad firmly in place to attach it to the first maxi pad, with the attached sections of the shoelaces sandwiched between them.

7. Place the maxi pad mask over your eyes, and tie the shoelaces behind your head to hold the eye mask in place.

HOW IT WORKS

The adhesive strips hold the maxi pads and shoelaces together, and the resulting sleep mask is both comfortably padded and thick enough to block out surrounding light.

DREAM ON

In South Korea, the most sleep-deprived nation of 18 developed countries, many long-distance commuters nap during their morning subway ride. In 2015, Burger King, which has 202 restaurants in South Korea, offered sleep masks to commuters at five major subway stations in Seoul. Printed across each sleep mask was a message asking other commuters to wake the wearer up in time for his stop. Each mask came with two coupons for free coffee at Burger King, so the wearer could use one coupon and share the other with the person who woke him up.

OFF THE BEATEN TRACK

How to Earn Tons of Frequent Flyer Miles

- Use a credit card that offers frequent flyer miles for every purchase you make. Charging nearly every purchase you make to the credit card (groceries, electric bill, entertainment)—and then paying the credit card bill in full every month—gives you tons of miles.
- Sign up for airline newsletters. These mailings offer all sorts of deals and promotions to give you extra miles.
- Sign up for a credit card that offers anywhere between 40,000 and 100,000 frequent flyer miles just for signing up and waives the annual fee for the first year. Be sure to read the fine print to rule out any hidden fees.
- Consider the monetary advantages of getting an airline credit card that offers free checked luggage.
- Try to fly one airline consistently to help you rack up miles on that frequent flyer program. Otherwise, you'll be earning miles on a number of airlines, never accumulating enough miles for a free flight.
- Monitor your frequent flyer accounts and record the expiration dates for miles you have acquired. You can extend the expiration dates by simply making a purchase of an item you intended to purchase anyway from a retail store through the airline's website.

How to Improvise Earplugs with Tampons

WHAT YOU NEED
- 2 appropriately sized tampons (such as o.b. Tampons)

WHAT TO DO
1. Unwrap the cellophane wrapper from the tampons, insert the ends of the tampons into your ears, and adjust them to fit snugly.
2. The tampons come equipped with convenient strings that make removal a snap. The strings also give the tampons a decorative touch, like fancy earrings.

HOW IT WORKS
The compressed cotton creates a somewhat effective sound barrier.

SOUND OFF
- In 1974, *Rolling Stone* reported that an inebriated John Lennon, attending the Troubadour nightclub in Los Angeles to see soul singer Ann Peebles, ended up with a tampon stuck to his forehead. "Don't you know who I am?" Lennon reportedly asked a waitress. "Yes," replied the waitress. "You're some asshole with a Kotex on his forehead."
- A British man who stuffed two tampons up his nose to try to stop his snoring suffocated in his sleep on January 23, 1996. After drinking wine and taking a few sleeping pills, Mark Gleeson, 26, of Headley Down, Hampshire—encouraged by his girlfriend, Tracey Lambert—stuck two of her tampons up his nose and secured them with tape before going to sleep on her sofa.
- In the 2006 movie *She's the Man*, Viola (Amanda Bynes) masquerades as her brother Sebastian and attends school in his place. When Sebastian's roommates find tampons in her bag, Viola (disguised as Sebastian) claims to use them to control "really bad nosebleeds."
- In an episode of *Curb Your Enthusiasm* ("The Divorce," season 8, episode 1) Larry David instructs a Girl Scout how to use a tampon. Later in the episode, David gets punched in the nose and deals with the resulting nosebleed by inserting a tampon into his nostril.

EVERY TRICK IN THE BOOK

Tampons Tricks

Tampons have plenty of hidden uses:

- **Clean Eyeglasses.** Rubbing the lenses of eyeglasses with a tampon cleans them beautifully. The cotton absorbs grease and grime, without leaving behind any lint.
- **Deodorize Shoes.** Place a tampon dampened with vinegar inside each shoe or sneaker overnight. By morning, odors will be gone.
- **Deodorize Your Car.** Instead of using a pine-scented tree, dampen a tampon with vinegar and hang it from your rearview mirror by the convenient string.
- **Improvise a Toothbrush.** In a pinch, a tampon can be used as a toothbrush.
- **Repel Moles or Gophers.** Saturate a tampon with ammonia, insert the engorged cotton deeply into the tunnel opening, and fill the tunnel with dirt. The pungent fumes will prompt the animals to tunnel elsewhere.
- **Shine Shoes.** To shine shoes, use the cotton tip of a tampon to buff. Many soldiers in the United States military buff their shoes and boots with tampons to achieve an impressive shine for inspections.
- **Stop Wounds from Bleeding.** Use a tampon as a compress for wounds or lacerations to control heavy bleeding. In an emergency, you can hold the tampon in place by tying it with string or duct tape.

How to Sleep on a Plane with a Beach Ball

WHAT YOU NEED
- An inflatable beach ball, 20-inch diameter (uninflated)
- Sweatshirt, sweater, or T-shirt (optional)

WHAT TO DO
1. Put your tray table down.
2. Inflate the beach ball and secure the nozzle shut.
3. If desired, place the inflated beach ball inside a sweatshirt, sweater, or T-shirt.
4. Place the beach ball on the tray table with the nozzle facing the surface.
5. Wrap your arms around the beach ball to hold it in place, and rest your head on the beach ball as a pillow.

HOW IT WORKS
The beach ball provides sufficient elevation from the tray table (approximately 14 inches) and keeps your body in a comfortable position for sleeping when you rest your head on the cushion. To decrease the height and soften the pillow, just let a little air out of the inflated beach ball.

SWEET DREAMS
- A beach ball can be used as a pillow of any size, a back support, or a seat cushion on a plane, train, or bus ride. It also makes a great play toy to entertain children anywhere in the world.
- Concertgoers, crowds at sporting events, and graduates at commencement ceremonies often volley beach balls around the crowd.
- Trained seals can frequently balance a beach ball on their noses.
- A beach ball can be used to play volleyball or water polo.
- Several American cities have painted their water towers to resemble a beach ball, including Hallandale Beach, Florida; Pensacola Beach, Florida; and Ocean City, Maryland.
- The multicolored wait cursor that appears in Apple's Mac operating system when the computer takes longer than usual to execute a certain task is often known as the "spinning beach ball of death."

How to Deodorize Flatulence with Whiskey

WHAT YOU NEED
- Mini-bottle of whiskey
- Napkin, bandana, coffee filter, or maxi pad

WHAT TO DO
1. If anonymous passengers in your vicinity expel gas, stinking up the surrounding area, purchase a mini-bottle of whiskey from a flight attendant and ask for a napkin.

2. Dampen the napkin with some whiskey, hold it over your nose, and breathe through the napkin.

HOW IT WORKS
Whiskey masks the scent of the sulfur compounds responsible for the foul-smelling odor of intestinal gas.

CREATING A STINK
- The average individual passes gas between 13 and 21 times a day.
- Changes in air pressure cause the digestive system to generate more gas.

- Many airplane passengers, intimated by their proximity to other people and the social stigma associated with releasing gas, attempt to hold in their flatulence. However, five gastroenterologists from Denmark and Britain published a study in the *New Zealand Medical Journal* in 2013 reporting that stifling the natural process "holds significant drawbacks for the individual such as discomfort and even pain, bloating, dyspepsia and pyrosis just to name but a few resulting abdominal symptoms."
- Women's farts tend to smell more odiferous than men's.

OFF THE BEATEN TRACK

How to Buy a Cheap Plane Ticket

Here are surefire secrets to booking cheap airfares:

- **Book Six Weeks in Advance.** A study by the Airlines Reporting Corporation in 2012 revealed that passengers who buy their ticket six weeks before their flight pay the lowest price, nearly 6 percent below the average fare.
- **Consider Buying Your Ticket on Tuesday at 3:00 PM EST.** On this day and time airlines release the most sales, according to a study by Farecompare.com, although the day and time of the best deals can vary widely.
- **Buy Your Airline Tickets During the Best Time Frame.** For domestic fares in the United States, buy your ticket between 3 months and 30 days before departure. For international fares, buy your ticket between 5½ months and 1½ months before departure.
- **Fly on Tuesdays, Wednesday, and Saturdays.** Tuesdays, Wednesdays, and Saturdays are usually the cheapest days to fly because fewer people wish to fly on those days, according to Rick Seaney, chief executive of farecompare.com.
- **Avoid Flying on Fridays and Sundays.** Fridays and Sundays are the most expensive days to fly, says Seaney. Vacation travelers like to head out early on Friday after work, and business travelers like to head out to Monday-morning meetings a day early, on Sunday.
- **Consider the Cheapest Times to Fly.** The red-eye and flights that take off at the crack of dawn are the least popular and, consequently, the least expensive.
- **Check Low-Cost Airlines Separately.** Comparison sites like Kayak do not always include budget airlines like Southwest and Ryanair.
- **Consider Extra Fees.** Before buying your ticket, be sure to calculate the baggage fees that may boost your cost.
- **Compare Connecting Flights to Nonstop Flights.** A flight with one or more stops along the way can save you as much as 50 percent off the ticket price.
- **Shop for Each Passenger Separately.** When the airline sells multiple tickets in a single transaction, the airline reservation system charges each ticket at the same price. In other words, if you shop for two people, and there is one ticket left for $100 but

several tickets available for $200, you'll pay $200 for each ticket. But if you book the seats separately, you'll pay $100 for the first ticket and $200 for the second, saving $100.

- **Fly into Larger Airports.** Airlines offer cheaper fares to hubs and large airports. Instead of flying in and out of a small local airport, compare the price of driving a few hours to or from a larger airport.

How to Make a Diaper out of a Maxi Pad and a Hand Towel

WHAT YOU NEED
- Maxi pad
- Airline blanket (or hand towel or pillow case)
- Safety pins (or duct tape)

WHAT TO DO
1. Place the blanket on a flat surface, fold it into a square, and then fold the square in half diagonally to form a right triangle. (The longest side of the triangle is the hypotenuse; the angle of the triangle opposite the hypotenuse is 90°.)

2. Peel off the adhesive strip from the back of the maxi pad, and adhere the maxi pad to the blanket to bisect the triangle along the imaginary line between the midpoint of the hypotenuse and the apex of the 90° angle.
3. Lay the baby with his crotch centered on the maxi pad on top of the blanket and facing the 90° angle of the triangle.
4. Fold the bottom end (the 90° angle of the triangle) of the blanket over the baby's belly.
5. Use safety pins to attach the back corners of the folded blanket to the front corners. (Or wrap strips of duct tape like a belt around the blanket to hold the makeshift diaper together.)

HOW IT WORKS
The blanket holds the absorbent maxi pad against the baby's bottom, and the maxi pad will soak up the bulk of any discharge.

OFF THE BEATEN TRACK

How to Avoid Getting Sick on a Plane

- To prevent getting infected with bacteria when you fly, bring along a 3-ounce bottle of alcohol-based hand sanitizer and a small pack of disinfectant wipes. When you take your seat, wipe down the armrests and tray table. According to a study conducted by Auburn University in Alabama, the highest levels of bacteria on a plane can be found on the chair upholstery, the tray table, the armrests, the toilet handle, the seat belts, the seatback pocket, the remote control, the window shade, and the door handles of the bathroom.
- Do not use the airline pillows or blankets. The unwashed pillowcases and blankets transmit germs. Instead, bring a sweater or jacket to stay warm. Use a blanket only if it's sealed in a plastic bag. If you bring you own neck pillow, be sure to launder it at home afterward.
- If you need to use the bathroom on a long-haul flight, do so early into the flight, rather than after several hours in the air. The bathroom gets filthier as the flight progresses because no one cleans them during the flight.
- Stay hydrated.
- Use a tissue or a paper towel to open bathroom doorknobs and touch toilet handles.
- Avoid touching your eyes with your fingers. Tear ducts provide the quickest route for germs to get to the nose and throat.
- Do not worry about the air in the cabin. The aircraft is equipped with HEPA (High Efficiency Particulate Air) filters, which remove bacteria and viruses from the air.
- Wearing a surgical mask will not protect you from Ebola or other serious diseases. Surgical masks are also generally ineffective at preventing colds and flu. The masks help prevent surgeons from spreading bacteria and contaminating patients, but do not protect the surgeons themselves from infection, as germs can enter through the mask. Surgical masks need to be changed every two hours to avoid contamination.

How to Entertain Noisy Kids with an Airsick Bag

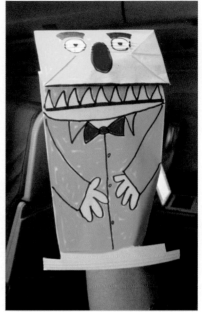

WHAT YOU NEED
- Airsick bag
- Indelible markers or crayons

WHAT TO DO

1. Lay the paper bag on the tray table with the opening of the bag facing toward you and the folded bottom of the bag facing up. The bottom will become your puppet's face.

2. Use the indelible markers or crayons to draw an upper lip just above the flap created by the bottom of the bag and a lower lip on the side of the bag just below the flap.

3. Draw facial features (eyes, nose, hair, mustache, etc.) above the flap on the folded bottom of the bag.

4. Open the flap created by the bottom of the bag to find the space between the upper and lower lip that will become the inside of your puppet's mouth. Draw teeth, a tongue, or anything else you choose.

5. Draw clothing, arms, and hands below the flap on the side of the bag.

6. To use the puppet, insert your hand into the bag and place your fingers in the flap. Move your fingers up and down to make the mouth move while you do the talking.

7. Make two or more hand puppets, giving you the ability to act out a story or put on a play.

HOW IT WORKS

Any paper bag can be made into a unique puppet, providing hours of entertainment for kids.

BAG OF TRICKS

- In 1949, inventor Gilmore Tilmen Schjeldahl created the world's first plastic-lined airsick bag—for Northwest Orient Airlines. Previously, airsick bags had been made from waxed paper. In his basement at home in Chicago, Schjeldahl and his wife, Charlene, discovered how to cut and seal sheets of polyethylene with hot knives. With a $100 investment, he went into business making polyethylene bags for packaging, eventually manufacturing an airsick bag with a plastic liner.

- Songwriter Nick Cave wrote an entire book on the back of airsick bags, an epic poem he started writing at the beginning of his 22-city tour in 2014 with his band the Bad Seeds. *The Sick Bag Song*, published in 2014 and described by the *New York Times* as "a mash-up of prose, poetry, song lyrics, and autobiography," includes full-color reproductions of the airsick bags adorned with Cave's scribbles.

- At the 1999 Aircraft Owners and Pilots Association Convention in Atlantic City, the Summit Bank of Wayne, New Jersey, determined to promote its low interest rates for aviation financing, handed out free barf bags printed with the headline SICK OF HIGH RATES?

- In 2000, British graphic designer Oz Dean, founder of the Australian design firm forcefeed:swede, created Design for Chunks, an annual online competition for artists to design innovative airsick bags. "I was intrigued to see how other designers would illustrate the usually plain in-flight sickbag," wrote Dean. The project quickly achieved cult status among graphic designers, and in 2004, Virgin Atlantic airlines, realizing the promotional value of the bags, issued a limited-edition set of 20 differently designed bags, printing half a million bags.

- If you're looking for something entertaining to do during a long flight, the 2009 book *Barfbag Origami* by Chris Marks gives step-by-step instructions on how to use the ancient Japanese art of paper folding to create a work of art from the airsick bag taken from the seatback pocket in front of you. The book features "Twenty-Seven First-Class Gags to Get Your Creative Juices Flowing."

- Guinness World Records recognizes Dutchman Niek Vermeulen as having the largest collection of airsick bags in the world, with 6,290 different bags from 1,191 different airlines as of February 28, 2012.

SICK JOKES

Here are a few other ways you can entertain yourself with an airsick bag:

- **Play "Mystery Quest."** One passenger covertly places an object into the airsick bag and seals it shut. The second passenger must guess the contents solely by feeling or shaking the bag.
- **Rubbings.** Place a coin or similar flat object inside the airsick bag. Rub a crayon on the bag to create a full-scale facsimile of the item.
- **Trick or Treat.** Color the airsick bag with Halloween decorations, and send your child trick-or-treating up and down the aisle and to the flight attendants in the galley.

OFF THE BEATEN TRACK
How to Choose the Best Seat on Any Plane

- The section of the plane in front of the engines is generally quietest in terms of engine noise.
- The rear of the cabin tends to get the most engine noise and the bumpiest ride if the plane encounters turbulence.
- Flights that are not fully booked tend to have more empty seats at the back of the plane, giving you more room to stretch out.
- For sleeping and fewer disturbances, a window seat provides the comfort of a cabin wall. However, the curvature of the cabin wall may impede shoulder room.
- The middle seat is considered the worst seat because you're sandwiched between two passengers who may elbow you recurrently.
- The aisle seat gives you more freedom to move about the cabin, but passengers and crew members walking past tend to bump into you, and you'll have to get out of your seat to let the passengers seated in your row use the restroom.
- A seat in an exit row gives you more legroom, but your tray table and video screen will be stored in the armrest.
- A bulkhead seat, located immediately behind a wall, offers more legroom and the luxury of having no seat that might recline in front of you. The tray table and video screen will be stored in the armrest.
- Seats near a restroom may put you in striking distance of irksome odors and the noise of the toilet flush. Passengers continually line up in the aisle to use the restroom, and when the lights in the cabin are darkened so passengers can sleep, every time a passenger opens the restroom door, bright light is emitted.
- Seats near the galleys generally suffer from more foot traffic, noise, and bright light.

How to Give Yourself a Foot Massage with Golf Balls

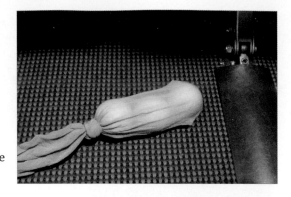

WHAT YOU NEED
- Scissors
- Pair of panty hose
- 3 to 6 golf balls

WHAT TO DO

1. Before leaving for the airport, use scissors to carefully cut off one leg of the pair of panty hose at the knee. Leave the scissors at home.
2. Insert the golf balls into the panty hose leg.
3. Tie a knot in the open end to secure the balls inside the panty hose leg.
4. Remove your shoes and place them under the seat in front of you.
5. Place the panty hose leg on the floor beneath your feet.
6. Roll one foot at a time over the golf balls.

HOW IT WORKS
The golf balls inside the panty hose leg massage your feet, and the nylon panty hose leg prevents the balls from scattering and getting lost.

THERE'S THE RUB
- You can also use three tennis balls and a sock to create both a back massager and foot massager.
- More people play golf than any other outdoor sport.
- Golf balls always spin backward when struck, which, if the balls were smooth, would create higher air pressure above the ball, preventing it from traveling more than 70 yards. Dimples in the ball carry air upward over the top, creating low air pressure over the ball, allowing it to be driven up to 300 yards.
- At the center of most golf balls is a sac filled with a liquid substance, usually castor oil and liquid silicone.

- Some farmers in Australia place golf balls under nesting hens to coax the chickens into thinking their eggs have not been taken so they'll lay more. But in 2008, in New South Wales, a 32-inch-long carpet python mistook the golf balls for eggs and swallowed four of them. Veterinarians at the Currumbin Wildlife Sanctuary x-rayed the snake and, deciding that the reptile would not pass the golf balls naturally, surgically removed them.

EVERY TRICK IN THE BOOK
Got Balls?

Here are some other uses for golf balls.

- **Coat Rack.** Drill a hole through the center of a few golf balls, and use 2-inch screws to attach the balls (spaced a few inches apart) to a plank of wood to create a stylish coat rack.
- **Drain Stopper.** If you can't find the plug, block the drain with a golf ball (first making certain the opening is smaller than the ball to avoid getting a golf ball stuck in the pipe). The suction created by the water pressure holds the golf ball in place, and the golf ball prevents the water from draining from the sink or tub.
- **Garden Edging.** Push a bunch of golf balls into the soil around your flowerbeds or vegetable garden or along your garden footpath to create beautiful edging.
- **Jacks Ball.** If you can't find the small, red rubber ball used for playing jacks, a golf ball makes an excellent substitute.
- **Picnic Tablecloth Weights.** To prevent the wind from blowing a picnic tablecloth off the table, fold back each of the four corners of the tablecloth and sew each triangular pocket around its own golf ball. The weight of the golf balls will help hold the tablecloth to the table.
- **Potted Plant Drainage.** Line the bottom of a plant pot with some golf balls, add potting soil, and situate your plant. The golf balls allow water to drain without dirt escaping from the pot.
- **Vase Filler.** Plunk several golf balls inside a vase to provide stabilizing weight, add some uniqueness to the decor, and hold the flowers in place.

3

HOTELS AND HOVELS

You're asleep in your hotel room when you're suddenly jolted from slumber by the sound of a family of 12 rolling their squeaky-wheeled luggage past your door. They burst into the room next door, the kids slamming doors and drawers, jumping on the bed, blasting the television, and tossing a tennis ball against the paper-thin walls. Eventually, Dad yells for the kids to pipe down and Mom tells them to get in bed, which provokes screaming and crying. When everything finally quiets down, you become painfully aware of the drip-drip-drip of the bathroom sink. Do you reach for the dental floss?

How to Seal the Curtains Shut with Clothes Hangers

WHAT YOU NEED

- 3 clothes hangers from your hotel room closet

WHAT TO DO

1. Close the curtains.
2. Hold the ends of the curtains together so they overlap.
3. Clip the clips from the first hanger in place over the curtains to hold them closed.
4. Repeat with a second and third hanger, making sure the curtains are securely shut.

HOW IT WORKS

Although they're attached to the hangers, the clips work to hold the curtains shut, and the weight of the hangers is not enough to pull the clips down from the curtains.

EVERY TRICK IN THE BOOK

It's Curtains for You

You can hold curtains together with these clips:

- **Binder Clips.** If you're traveling on a business trip with documents held together with binder clips, those small metallic clasps work beautifully to hold hotel room curtains shut.
- **Claw Hair Clips.** While not as effective as other clips, these talon-like clips work magic in a pinch.
- **Paper Clips.** As long as the air-conditioning unit doesn't blow a powerful breeze up under the closed curtains, paper clips may work wonders to keep those curtains sealed tight.
- **Potato Chip Bag Clips.** These long, strong plastic clips firmly grip the curtains together and keep them closed.
- **Snap-in Hair Clips.** These slender clips are sturdy enough to hold the two sides of the curtains together, depending on the thickness of the fabric.

OFF THE BEATEN TRACK

Rules of the Road

- Always keep the Do Not Disturb sign on the outside doorknob of your hotel room, even when you're out of the room. This prevents housekeeping from entering your room.
- Always wear flip-flops in the shower to avoid getting athlete's foot or plantar warts.
- Use sanitizer wipes to clean the phone and television remote control, the places most apt to house germs.
- Place a hand towel on the bathroom counter to lay out your toiletry items (or keep them in your toiletry kit).
- When you're in your room, keep the door locked, including the security locks.
- Never open your door without using the peephole first to verify the person's identity.
- If you find yourself in the middle of a catastrophe, fill the bathtub with water, and then go to the hotel bar and buy all the bottles of liquor. The filled bathtub becomes your emergency water supply, and you can use the alcohol as an anesthetic, an antiseptic, fuel to start a fire, or—should the economy completely collapse—the new currency.

How to Hide Money in a Toilet Paper Holder

WHAT YOU NEED
- Toilet paper holder in your hotel room

WHAT TO DO
1. Remove the toilet paper from the holder.
2. Take the holder apart.
3. Roll up your money tightly.
4. Slip the money roll inside the spring.
5. Place the spring back inside the toilet paper holder, and reassemble the two parts.
6. Place the toilet paper back on the holder.

HOW IT WORKS
The toilet paper holder conceals the money contained within, and despite being filled with a roll of currency, the roll of toilet paper continues to function properly when used.

LET'S ROLL
If the toilet paper dispenser in the bathroom holds a second roll of toilet paper in a compartment behind the first "active" roll, remove the first roll from the holder, shove your money inside the hollow tube of the second roll, and replace the first roll on the holder.

EVERY TRICK IN THE BOOK

More Great Places to Hide Your Money in a Hotel Room

Where can you hide your money at home or when you're on the go?

- **Curtain Rods.** Remove the decorative finial from one end of a curtain rod, roll up the bills, and insert them into the hollow rod. Then replace the decorative finial.

- **Drop-Ceiling Tiles.** Slide open a ceiling tile in a drop ceiling, place a small bag or box of money or valuables atop the tile, and place the ceiling tile back in position.
- **Ironing Board.** Remove the ironing board from the closet, pull back the fabric cover from the ironing board, and place several bills flat between the metal ironing board top and the fabric cover. Replace the cover and put the ironing board back in the closet.

- **Night Table.** Lift up the night table an inch from the ground, and slide your money underneath.
- **Tissue Box.** Remove the faceplate from a tissue box mounted in the side of a bathroom countertop, place your money behind the tissue box, and replace the faceplate.
- **Towels.** If housekeeping keeps the hand towels folded with a fancy pocket, hide your money in the pocket behind the fanned washcloth.

How to Defog a Bathroom Mirror with Shaving Cream

WHAT YOU NEED
- Shaving cream
- Washcloth

WHAT TO DO
1. Fill your palm with a handful of shaving cream.
2. Rub the shaving cream on the mirror over the sink where you normally look when brushing your teeth, brushing your hair, applying makeup, or shaving.
3. Using the washcloth, wipe the shaving cream off the mirror.

HOW IT WORKS
The thin coat of shaving cream emollients left on the mirror prevents the steam created by the shower from fogging up the glass. The effect can last up to three weeks.

MIRROR, MIRROR ON THE WALL
- Don't have shaving cream? Apply a few drops of shampoo on the mirror with a washcloth, and then wipe clean with a hand towel.
- You can also dry steam from a fogged-up bathroom mirror in a hotel room by using the provided blow dryer to blow hot air at the mirror. The hot air helps the steam evaporate from the mirror.

FOR YOUR EYES ONLY
Step into a steamy bathroom while wearing your eyeglasses, and they're sure to get fogged up. The solution?
- **Deodorant.** Spraying both sides of the eyeglass lenses with deodorant and then wiping them clean prevents the lenses from fogging up.
- **Shampoo.** Rub a small drop of shampoo on both sides of the eyeglass lenses, and then wipe them clean. The thin film of soap left behind prevents the lenses from fogging up—just like the mirror.
- **Shaving Cream.** Keep eyeglasses from fogging up by rubbing a small dab of shaving cream over both sides of the eyeglass lenses and then wiping them clean. The residual film of condensed soap prevents the lenses from fogging up—again, just like the mirror.

- **Toothpaste.** To prevent a pair of eyeglasses from fogging up, wipe both sides of the lenses clean with a dab of regular toothpaste. Scuba divers commonly use toothpaste to prevent their swim mask from fogging up underwater. Use only regular toothpaste on eyeglasses. Tartar control or whitening toothpastes can damage plastic.

OFF THE BEATEN TRACK
How to Get a Free Hotel Room Upgrade

- **Just Ask—Politely and Discreetly.** Be nice to the people at the front desk and ask if there's any possibility for a better room. The underappreciated people at the front desk hold the power to give you something more. Do not ask within earshot of other guests. Otherwise, the person at the front desk will say no solely to prevent a chain reaction.
- **Announce a Special Occasion.** If you're celebrating a birthday, anniversary, graduation, or other special event, let the front desk know and ask if there's anything special they can do to help enhance the occasion.
- **Enroll in the Hotel's Loyalty Program.** Being a member shows that you're a frequent guest and will make the front desk clerk more inclined to upgrade you to a better room.
- **Check in Late.** The later you check into the hotel, the better the front desk will know which rooms are available that night.
- **Contact a New Hotel.** A newly opened hotel, eager to attract new guests, may be more willing to offer upgrades to foster loyalty and generate good word-of-mouth publicity.
- **Book a Mid-Range Room.** If you're willing to pay for a room a notch above the basic accommodation, the front desk is more apt to upgrade you to a higher level.

How to Soundproof Your Hotel Room with a Bath Towel

WHAT YOU NEED
- Bath towel

WHAT TO DO
1. Spread the towel on the floor or bed.
2. Roll up the towel lengthwise.
3. Place the towel roll on the floor against the base of the door to cover up the space created between the bottom of the door and the floor.
4. Whenever you leave the room and return again, place the towel back in position.

HOW IT WORKS
The space created between the bottom of the door and floor allows sound waves outside the room to travel into your room. Placing the thick roll against the space blocks the sound waves.

SLEEP TIGHT
Want to get a good night's sleep in a hotel room?
- **Do Your Homework.** Before making a reservation at a hotel, make sure the hotel is not being renovated and that no construction projects are underway within earshot.
- **Make Reservations at a Soundproof or Noise-Sensitive Hotel.** Some hotels have been designed with special flooring to reduce and deaden sound. Others designate certain floors as quiet zones, forbidding children and social groups, and providing guests with nightlights, blackout curtains, drape clips, sleep CDs, eye masks, earplugs, and sleep-inducing aromatic sprays.
- **Consider Airport Hotels.** Upscale hotels near airports are generally built with super soundproofing to mute the roar of jet engines.

- **Bring Earplugs.** You can always sandwich your head between two pillows, but earplugs reduce noise by around 33 decibels—far more than a pillow.
- **Request a Quiet Room When You Check In.** Ask for a room on an upper floor, facing away from the street, without a door to an adjoining room, and away from the elevators, vending machines, ice machines, a wedding party, conventioneers, or a roomful of fraternity brothers. When you go up to the room, make sure it suits your needs before settling in. If it doesn't, go back downstairs to reception and ask for another room.
- **Quell Noisy Neighbors.** If slamming doors, loud televisions, screaming, and pounding noises come through the walls or ceiling, do not confront the neighbors on your own (possibly exacerbating the situation or risking harm to yourself). Instead, call the front desk and ask them to handle the matter. The front desk will send security to make the offenders pipe down or risk being expelled from the hotel.
- **Call Maintenance.** If you hear the toilet running, the shower dripping, or the air conditioner clanking, call the front desk to send maintenance to fix it.
- **Ask for Another Room.** If the noise is beyond control, insist upon being changed to another room.
- **Turn Off or Reset the Alarm Clock.** Make sure the previous hotel room guest did not set the bedside alarm clock for 4:00 AM.
- **Place the DO NOT DISTURB Sign Outside the Door.** It may sound obvious, but unless you put the DO NOT DISTURB sign on your door, housekeepers will inevitably knock on your door in the morning when you're still sleeping.

OFF THE BEATEN TRACK

How to Get a Cheap Price on a Hotel Room

Here are some strategies for getting the best hotel rates whenever you travel:

- **Be Flexible with Dates.** Room rates can vary widely based on the days of week and time of year. Hotels catering to business travelers tend to offer discounted weekend rates, while vacation properties offer discounted midweek prices.
- **Avoid Tourist Season.** Plan your trip for a time of year when demand for rooms is low and supply is high.
- **Shop Around Online.** Compare the prices on websites like Hotels.com, Expedia, Orbitz, Travelocity, and Kayak to find the lowest rate, and then telephone the hotel directly to match the price.
- **Name Your Price.** If you're willing to book a hotel based on a general location and quality, bid for a hotel room on Priceline or Hotwire.
- **Ask for a Lower Rate.** Call up the hotel directly and ask for any promotions, packages, or special rates for AAA members, seniors, frequent flyers, or whatever groups you may belong to.
- **Cash In on Last-Minute Specials.** If you book your trip at the last minute during an off-season, the hotel managers may lower the price to fill empty rooms.
- **Book a Package Deal.** Booking your flight and hotel together as a package deal may save money.
- **Investigate Alternative Accommodations.** Consider bed-and-breakfasts or vacation rentals, which can be found on Airbnb.com and VRBO.com. Or try hostels at hihostels.com and hostels.com.
- **Consider Hidden Fees.** Don't be swayed by a low base rate without adding in the taxes, fees, and parking costs.
- **Use Coupon and Voucher Books.** Search the Internet for coupons for specific hotels, or use a discount coupon, and take advantage of an Entertainment Book membership (see Entertainment.com).
- **Use Loyalty Points.** You can use points accumulated with a hotel's loyalty program or a frequent flyer account to pay for a hotel room (or an upgrade).
- **Follow Up.** After you book a hotel reservation, call back or check online a few weeks later to check whether rates have dropped. If so, cancel your original reservation (provided you need not pay any penalties) and rebook at the lower rate.

How to Cook Hot Dogs in a Coffeemaker

WHAT YOU NEED
- Coffeemaker
- Water
- Knife
- Package of hot dogs
- Fork

WHAT TO DO
1. Fill the reservoir in the coffeemaker with water.
2. Using the knife, carefully cut the hot dogs in half to fit in the carafe, if necessary.
3. Place the hot dogs inside the glass carafe.
4. Turn on the coffeemaker. (Do not place a coffee filter or any coffee in the machine.)
5. After the water fills the carafe, let the hot dogs heat in the water for 45 minutes.
6. Using a fork, carefully fish the hot dogs from the hot water in the carafe.

HOW IT WORKS
The water, heated to roughly 205° Fahrenheit, begins cooking the hot dogs, and the hot plate, designed to keep the coffee warm, finishes the job.

HOT DOG!
If you don't have a coffeemaker, here are several other creative ways to cook a hot dog:
- **Electrocution.** Use wire cutters to carefully cut the cord from an unplugged lamp, separate the two wires for 6 inches, and strip ¾ inch of plastic coating off the end of each of the two wires. Wrap the exposed end of one wire around the end of one fork. Wrap the exposed end of the second wire around the end of a second fork. Insert each fork into an opposite end of the hot dog. Dangle the cord over the bottom

bar of a wooden coat hanger, and hang the prepared hanger so that *neither the hot dog nor the wired forks touch anything or anyone*. Place a towel under the hot dog to absorb any drips. Plug the cord into an outlet. The 110 watts of electricity will cook the hot dog in 1 to 2 minutes. Unplug the extension cord from the outlet and allow the forks to cool to the touch. To avoid electrocuting yourself, *never touch the forks or the hot dog until the cord is fully unplugged.*

- **Frying.** Lay a coat hanger across the mouth of a wastebasket, then carefully set a clothes iron on the hanger, handle side down, to create a stable, level ironing surface. Set the iron on "heat" with the steam setting turned off. Using a toothbrush or pocket comb as a spatula, fry the hot dog.

- **Grilling.** Straighten a wire clothes hanger to create a long metal skewer, insert the end through the hot dog lengthwise, and grill the frankfurter over a wood fire in a fireplace, rotating it slowly.

- **Solar Cooking.** Line the inside of a parabolic bowl (such as a colander) with aluminum foil (shiny side out). Suspend the hot dog on a skewer in the center of the bowl, and set outside in the sunshine for 60 to 90 minutes.

How to Use a Bathtub as a Washing Machine

WHAT YOU NEED

- Bathtub
- Drain Plug
- Water
- Shampoo (or laundry detergent)
- Wooden clothes hanger (optional)
- Bar of soap (optional)
- Hairbrush (optional)

WHAT TO DO

1. Plug the bathtub, and begin filling it with enough water (warm for separated colors, cold for mixed colors) to submerge the laundry load.
2. While the water is running, add 1 or 2 tablespoons of shampoo (depending on the amount of clothes) to the water or the appropriate amount of detergent based on instructions on the box.
3. With your hands, swish the water in the tub to create suds.
4. Submerge the laundry in the soapy water in the bathtub.
5. Let the laundry soak for 10 minutes.
6. Swirl with your hands (or a wooden clothes hanger) and knead the garments in the water for 5 minutes. Or step barefoot into the tub and walk over the clothes. For tough stains, rub the affected area with a bar of soap. If necessary, scrub stains with a hairbrush.
7. Drain the water from the bathtub and wring out the clothes, allowing the soapy water to empty down the drain.
8. Turn on the faucet and individually rinse each item of clothing under the running water, wringing out any soapy water. Toss each rinsed garment to the back end of the bathtub.
9. Plug the drain and fill the tub with enough cool water to submerge the clothes.
10. Using your hands (or a wooden clothes hanger), swirl the clothes in the water and wring out any lingering soap.

11. Drain the soapy water from the bathtub, allowing it to empty down the drain.

12. Turn on the faucet and individually rinse each item of clothing under the running water one last time, wringing out any residual soapy water.

13. Hang the wet clothes over the shower curtain rod, a retractable indoor clothesline installed in the bathtub stall, a clothesline fashioned from a piece of rope, or outside draped over a patio railing or patio chairs.

HOW IT WORKS

Agitating the dirty clothes in soapy water duplicates the action of a washing machine, and rinsing the soapy water from the garments with clean water mimics the rinse cycle. Depending on the temperature, humidity, and how well you wring the water from the clothes, the garments will be fully dry in anywhere from a few hours to two days.

ALL WASHED UP

- You can also use a clean, unused plunger to mimic the action of the agitator of a washing machine.
- To remove as much water as possible from the garment to speed drying time, lay a bath towel on a flat surface, lay the wet garment on top of the towel, and roll up the towel with the garment inside it. Walk along the rolled-up towel on your knees. Then unroll the garment and hang it (and the towel) up to dry. The towel absorbs excess water from the garment.
- Running the exhaust fan in the bathroom hastens drying time (but wastes electricity).

How to Silence a Dripping Sink with Dental Floss

WHAT YOU NEED

- Dental floss (or a shoelace)

WHAT TO DO

1. Cut off a piece of dental floss long enough to reach from the end of the spout to the drain in the sink.
2. Tie one end of the dental floss around the end of the spout.
3. Place the free end of the dental floss so it touches the bottom of the sink.
4. Position the knot under the aerator at the tip of the faucet so that the dripping water flows down the string to the bottom of the sink.

HOW IT WORKS

The drips of water slide down the dental floss and then run off into the drain—silently. Water has both cohesive and adhesive properties, meaning it sticks to itself (cohesion) and other items, like string (adhesion).

NO STRINGS ATTACHED

- A sponge placed under a leaky faucet will silently catch the drips as well.
- In Robert Pirsig's novel *Zen and the Art of Motorcycle Maintenance*, the narrator shares his friend John's philosophy on a dripping faucet: "If you try to fix a faucet and your fixing doesn't work, then it's just your lot to live with a dripping faucet." The narrator soon discovers that John's wife "was suppressing anger at that faucet and that goddamned dripping faucet was just about killing her!"
- In the 1965 horror film *Repulsion*, directed by Roman Polanski, Carol (Catherine Deneuve) hallucinates the disproportionately loud sounds of a dripping faucet.
- In the *Twilight Zone* episode "Sounds and Silences" (season 5, episode 27), Roswell Flemington (John McGiver) wakes up to the sound of a dripping bathroom faucet, but to him, each drop sounds like a gunshot.

How to Improvise a Bathtub Stopper with a Tennis Ball

WHAT YOU NEED
- Tennis ball
- Bathtub (or sink)
- Water

WHAT TO DO
1. Place the tennis ball in the drain, and hold it in place to form a tight seal.
2. Begin filling the bathtub with water.
3. Once the water level covers the tennis ball, release the ball.
4. Continue filling the bathtub with water to the desired level.

HOW IT WORKS
The water pressure and the resulting suction from the drain hold the beveled edge of the tennis ball securely in the drain, despite the fact that the rubber ball is buoyant enough to float.

DOWN THE DRAIN
- If you don't have a tennis ball, saturate five sheets of paper towel with water, wring out the excess, bunch the towels into a ziplock bag, and seal it shut. Wedge the bag into the drain.
- Place a circular plastic lid from a margarine container or plastic kitchen container over the drain, and the water pressure will hold the lid in place.
- If you've lost the stopper for the drain in the bathtub or sink, fill a ziplock freezer bag with water, seal it shut, and place it over the drain hole. The suction from the drain will hold the plastic bag in place, corking the drain.
- An unused Keurig cup fits in most drains and makes an excellent substitute for a drain stopper that can be easily removed.

How to Hide Valuables in a Comfy Chair

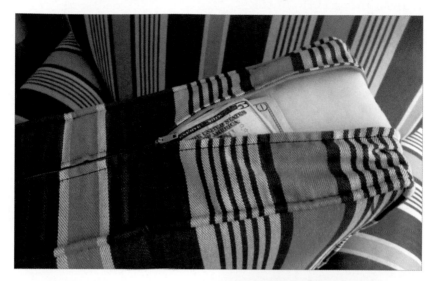

WHAT YOU NEED

- Valuables
- A comfy chair

WHAT TO DO

1. Remove the seat cushion from the comfy chair.
2. Locate the zipper in the back of the cushion and slide it open.
3. Place your valuables or money inside the cushion and zip it closed again.
4. Place the seat cushion back in position in the comfy chair.

HOW IT WORKS

The zippered chair cushion provides a concealed cavity for hiding money or other valuables.

PULL UP A CHAIR

In her book *You Only Die Once*, author Margie Jenkins writes that when her father's uncle died, her parents searched his home and found large quantities of cash "under the mattress, tucked into books, inside chair cushion covers, among bed linens in the closet, behind canned food on pantry shelves, and in a jelly jar in the refrigerator."

OFF THE BEATEN TRACK

How to Book a Room in a Sold-Out Hotel

Want a room at a fully booked hotel? You just need to understand the hotel's policies, exert a bit of effort, and refuse to take no for an answer.

- **Be Polite.** Hotel managers and reservation clerks will be more inclined to help you if you treat them respectfully and with kindness.
- **Use the Cancellation Policy to Your Advantage.** Find out what time the hotel's cancellation penalties take effect for the date you wish to check in (usually 24 hours in advance), and call the hotel just after that time to grab a room made available by a cancellation.
- **Go Through an Online Reservation Website.** Many hotels sell blocks of rooms to online websites like Travelocity.com and Expedia.com, and then list them as booked. The hotel may appear fully booked through the hotel, but rooms may still be available through the ancillary website.
- **Telephone the Hotel Directly.** The national 800 number for a hotel may have a limit on the number of rooms they book. The front desk at an individual hotel in the chain may have more rooms set aside.
- **Ask the Front Desk at the Hotel to Put Your Name on a Waiting List for Rooms.** Hotels frequently get last-minute cancellations, and people on the waiting list get offered these last-minute rooms. Be sure to check back with the hotel persistently to see if any rooms have become available.
- **Make a Backup Plan.** If you can't get into your first choice, be sure you have a reservation at another hotel so you don't end up sleeping in your car.

How to Cook a Grilled Cheese Sandwich with an Iron

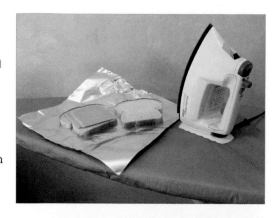

WHAT YOU NEED

- Clothes iron
- 2 slices of American cheese
- 2 slices of bread
- Aluminum foil

WHAT TO DO

1. Preheat the iron to the wool setting with the steam setting turned off.
2. Place two slices of American cheese between two slices of bread and wrap the sandwich in a sheet of aluminum foil.
3. Place the wrapped sandwich on a wooden cutting board or ironing board.
4. Place the hot iron on the top of the wrapped sandwich for 20 seconds.

5. Flip over the wrapped sandwich and place the hot iron on top of the other side for 20 seconds.
6. Carefully unwrap the grilled cheese sandwich and enjoy.

HOW IT WORKS

The soleplate of the iron doubles as a cooking grill, heating to 300° F on the wool setting, just the right amount of heat to toast the bread and melt the cheese.

IRON TEMPERATURES

The adjustable dial on irons to indicate the multiple temperature control settings for different types of fabric can be used to adjust the temperature for cooking. While irons made by different manufacturers tend to differ slightly in temperature, here are the approximate temperatures of common fabric settings.

- Linen: 445° F
- Cotton: 400° F
- Wool: 300° F
- Polyester: 300° F
- Silk: 300° F
- Acrylic: 275° F
- Nylon: 275° F

OFF THE BEATEN TRACK
How to Save Money at Restaurants

- **Don't Order Drinks.** Restaurants give the price of alcoholic beverages and soft drinks the highest markups, and the beverages you order could easily wind up costing more than your meal. Ask for a glass of water with a twist of lemon or lime. If you must have a cocktail or a glass of wine, do so at home before going out—making sure you have a designated driver. And instead of ordering coffee after the meal, brew a pot when you get home.
- **Visit Restaurants for Lunch Rather Than Dinner.** Items on the lunch menu are less expensive than those same items on the dinner menu.
- **Order an Appetizer Rather Than an Entrée.** If you're not hungry, order a low-cost appetizer from the menu as your main course, and be sure to ask the waiter for a basket of complimentary fresh bread, salad, or chips and salsa.
- **Share a Main Dish.** You can save 50 percent off the price of dinner at nearly any restaurant by simply sharing your meal with your dining companion. Just ask the waiter to bring an extra plate and some extra bread. Some restaurants charge a small fee for sharing a meal, but most don't mind since their portions tend to be so big. Be sure to tip well.
- **Catch the Early Bird Special.** Many restaurants—particularly in Florida near retirement communities—offer discounted dinner meals between 4:00 PM and 6:00 PM.
- **Clip Two-for-One Coupons.** Check the local Sunday newspaper, local area magazines in hotel racks for tourists, the yellow pages, restaurant websites, or www.valpak.com, www.moneymailer.com, or www.wow-coupons.com for coupons from restaurants offering discounts like two meals for the price of one (usually for up to four people).
- **"What's Today's Special?"** Before ordering from the menu, ask the waiter about any specials for the day that aren't listed on the menu. Most restaurants have regular daily specials, with the best deals running Monday through Thursday (rarely on weekends).
- **Snack Before You Dine.** Before going out to a restaurant, eat a light snack, like a piece of fruit, to make sure you're not famished. If you go to a restaurant on an empty stomach, your eyes will be larger than your stomach and you'll be more likely to order the most expensive item on the menu.

How to Shine Your Shoes with Lip Balm and a Coffee Filter

WHAT YOU NEED
- Lip balm
- Coffee filter (or maxi pad)

WHAT TO DO
1. Rub the lip balm on the shoes.
2. Buff with a coffee filter.

HOW IT WORKS
The carnauba wax, mineral oil, wax paraffin, and white wax in the lip balm work to revitalize the leather. The coffee filter, made from 100 percent virgin paper, buffs the wax without leaving behind any lint.

EVERY TRICK IN THE BOOK
If the Shoe Fits

You can also shine shoes with:

- **Body Lotion.** Apply a dab of body lotion to your shoes, rub with a soft cloth, and buff to a shine.
- **Furniture Polish.** Spray a bit of furniture polish on the shoes and buff with a coffee filter or maxi pad. The oils in the furniture polish clean and shine leather shoes.
- **Hair Gel.** Applying a dab of hair gel to the leather will give the shoes a reasonable shine. Rub with a soft cloth and buff.
- **Olive Oil.** Put a few drops of olive oil on a soft cloth and buff.
- **Stick Deodorant.** Apply stick deodorant to the leather, rub with a soft cloth, and buff.

How to Exfoliate Your Face and Legs with Sugar Packets

WHAT YOU NEED
- 3 sugar packets

WHAT TO DO
1. After shaving or washing your face, empty a packet of sugar into your cupped palm.
2. Add a few drops of water to the sugar and, using your fingers, mix a thick paste.
3. Using your fingertips, apply the paste to your wet skin, and massage lightly, drawing circles with your fingertips over your face, applying pressure appropriately, without scrubbing.
4. Rinse your face clean with water.
5. To exfoliate your legs, wet your legs.
6. Empty two or three packets of sugar into your cupped palm, and rub the sugar onto the tops of your legs with a circular motion, working gradually toward the bottom of your legs.
7. Rinse clean with water.

HOW IT WORKS
The sugar granules slough off the top layers of dead skin, leaving the skin with a healthy glow.

JUST A SPOONFUL OF SUGAR
- Sugar is a natural humectant, drawing moisture from the environment into the skin. In other words, when you apply sugar to the skin, it helps hydrate it.
- Sugar contains glycolic acid and alpha-hydroxy acids, which help remove the top layer of skin cells without scrubbing.
- Exfoliating the skin cells generates fresher, younger-looking skin.
- Sugar granules are more rounded than salt crystals, making them gentler and more suitable for sensitive skin. Salt scrubs can cause microscopic tears in the skin and strip the skin of natural oils.
- Brown sugar is softer than granulated sugar and better for use on the face. Raw sugar is more coarse than granulated, making it better for use on the body.

How to Dry Wet Shoes or Boots with Newspaper

WHAT YOU NEED
- Newspaper

WHAT TO DO
1. Drain as much water as possible from the shoes or boots.
2. Remove the insoles, if possible, and let them dry separately.
3. Crumple up individual sheets of newspaper and shove them inside the shoes or boots.
4. Continue shoving balls of crumpled newspaper into the shoes or boots until they are full of newspaper.
5. Let the footwear stand upside down overnight in a warm, dry area. If possible change the newspaper every hour.
6. Remove the crumpled-up sheets of newsprint and discard.
7. Repeat if necessary.

HOW IT WORKS
The newsprint absorbs the excess moisture from inside the shoes or boots.

YOU BET YOUR BOOTS
- Footwear dries faster when placed upside down.
- Another way to quickly dry shoes or boots: place them (with the insoles removed and the tongue propped open) in front of a fan in a room-temperature environment.
- Rice also absorbs moisture. Fill your footwear with uncooked rice, let it sit overnight, and then discard the rice. Or cut off the legs of a pair of clean, used panty hose, fill each foot with rice, tie a knot in the open end, and place one foot inside each shoe or boot overnight.
- Do not place wet footwear near a heat source, such as a fireplace, heater, campfire, radiator, or sunny windowsill. High heat can damage shoes and boots, weaken the adhesives, and harden the material, particularly leather.
- Do not allow wet shoes or boots to remain wet for a long period of time. Otherwise, mold will begin to grow inside them.

How to Clean Sneakers with Toothpaste

WHAT YOU NEED
- Toothpaste
- Sponge (or clean, used toothbrush)
- Glass of water
- Washcloth

WHAT TO DO
1. Squirt a small dab of toothpaste onto a sponge, and rub the toothpaste into the sneaker.
2. Dip the sponge into the glass of water and continue scrubbing the sneaker.
3. Blot with a wet washcloth.

HOW IT WORKS
The calcium, phosphate, glycerin, and sodium lauryl sulfate in toothpaste cleans the canvas of the sneaker.

CUT AND PASTE
Toothpaste can also be used to clean:
- **Burn Marks.** To clean minor burn marks from wood furniture, rub the spot with toothpaste, and then wipe clean with a soft, clean cloth.
- **Clothes Iron.** To clean residue from the silver soleplate on an iron, squeeze a dollop of toothpaste on a damp, soft cloth and rub the bottom of the *cool, unplugged iron*. Rinse well.
- **Compact Disc.** To stop a compact disc from skipping, rub a dab of toothpaste on the disk with a clean, soft cloth. Rinse clean with water, and dry thoroughly.
- **Crayon.** To clean crayon marks off walls, squeeze some toothpaste on an old toothbrush and scrub the marks.
- **Crayon, Lip Balm, or Lipstick**. If crayons or a tube of lip balm or lipstick go through the dryer, leaving melted wax all over the inside of the dryer, squeeze a dollop of toothpaste on a sponge, a stiff nail brush, or a clean, used toothbrush, and scrub the spots. Wipe clean with a damp rag.

- **Grout.** Squeeze a dollop of toothpaste on a clean, old toothbrush, and scrub the grout.
- **Hair Dye.** To remove hair dye from skin, apply a dollop of toothpaste on a damp cloth and rub the stained skin gently in a circular motion. Repeat if necessary.
- **Piano Keys.** To clean ivory or plastic piano keys, squeeze a dollop of toothpaste on a damp, soft, clean cloth, rub the keys, and wipe clean.
- **Porcelain.** To clean stubborn stains from a porcelain sink, squeeze a dab of toothpaste on a soft, clean cloth and rub the stains. Rinse clean and dry.
- **Scuff Marks.** To clean scuff marks from vinyl, linoleum, or tile floors, squeeze a dab of toothpaste on a damp, clean, soft cloth, and rub. Clean with a clean, wet cloth.
- **Silver.** To clean tarnish from silver, squeeze a dollop of toothpaste on a soft, clean cloth, and rub the item. Rinse and dry.
- **Tar.** To clean tar from skin, rub a dollop of toothpaste into the tar, and then rinse clean.
- **Water Spots.** To remove water spots from a penetrating-sealed wood floor, squeeze a dab of toothpaste on a damp, clean, soft cloth and rub the spot until the white mark disappears.
- **Water Rings.** To remove a white ring from wood furniture, squeeze a dab of toothpaste on a damp, clean, soft cloth and rub the ring until the white mark disappears.

How to Clean a Retainer in a Ziplock Freezer Bag

WHAT YOU NEED

- Ziplock freezer bag, sandwich size
- Water
- Denture cleansing tablets

WHAT TO DO

1. Rinse off the retainer with water to remove any visible buildup.
2. Place the retainer in the ziplock bag and fill the bag halfway with warm—not hot—water. (Hot water can distort the plastic.)
3. Add two denture cleansing tablets, and seal the bag shut.
4. Let it soak for 15 to 20 minutes.
5. Discard the liquid and remove the retainer from the bag.
6. Clean the retainer thoroughly with toothpaste and a toothbrush to remove any residual plaque. Rinse off the retainer.

HOW IT WORKS

When you wear a retainer for several hours, tartar and bacteria build up on the orthodontic device. Denture cleansing tablets, developed to remove tartar and bacteria from dentures, work equally well on retainers—and the instructions above can also be used to clean dentures in a ziplock bag.

HOW TO RETAIN YOUR RETAINER

- Never carry a retainer in your pocket or purse unprotected (not even in a plastic bag). Otherwise, the retainer may get damaged.
- Never wrap a retainer in a napkin or tissue. Otherwise, it might get thrown away accidentally.
- Never leave your retainer in a hot car, washing machine, or dishwasher.
- Never leave your retainer lying around (even in the case). Otherwise, your pets may chew on it or someone may step on it.
- Never boil a retainer in water or soak it in rubbing alcohol, mouthwash, bleach, or any other strong cleansing solution.
- Never store a retainer in the case without cleaning it. Otherwise the retainer will become stained, start to smell, and grow mold.

How to Make a Lint Brush from Packaging Tape

WHAT YOU NEED

- Packaging tape

WHAT TO DO

1. Wrap a strip of packaging tape around your hand with the sticky side out.
2. Pat your clothes with the tape.
3. Remove the strip of tape from your hand and discard.
4. Repeat with a fresh strip of tape if necessary.

HOW IT WORKS

The lint or pet hairs will stick to the tape.

EVERY TRICK IN THE BOOK

The Brush Off

Here are a few other ways to remove lint and pet hair from clothes:

- **Dryer Sheets.** To remove pet hair from clothes or furniture, simply wipe the affected area with a used dryer sheet, which works like a magnet, attracting all the hairs.
- **Latex Gloves.** To remove pet hair from clothes or furniture, put on a pair of latex gloves, fill a bucket halfway with water, dip the gloves in the water, wipe the area affected by the pet hair, and dip the gloves in the water again. The wet rubber attracts the pet hair, and the water in the bucket rinses it off.
- **Lemon Juice.** To prevent lint in the dryer, add ¼ cup lemon juice in the final rinse cycle of the washing machine.
- **Pair of Panty Hose.** When drying clothes covered with lint, toss a clean, used pair of panty hose into the dryer along with the linty clothes. The nylon works like a magnet, attracting all the lint.
- **Vinegar.** To avoid generating lint, add ½ cup of vinegar to the final rinse in the washing machine.

How to Electrocute an Intruder with a Table Lamp

WHAT YOU NEED

- Wire cutters (or scissors or knife)
- Table lamp
- Several glasses of water

WHAT TO DO

1. If an intruder threatens to break into your room and cause you physical harm, use the wire cutters to cut the end of the cord from the lamp.
2. Separate the two wires for the length of the cord.
3. Using the wire cutters, strip roughly 5 inches of plastic coating off the end of the active (hot) wire. The wire connected to the smaller blade of the plug is the active (hot) wire.

4. Attach the stripped end of the active wire to the doorknob by wrapping it securely around the handle. Make certain that the wire cannot fall off the doorknob.
5. Using the wire cutters, strip 1 inch of plastic coating off the end of the second (neutral) wire.
6. Attach the stripped end of the second wire to the carpet directly beneath the doorknob.
7. Pour several glasses of water beneath the door to make a large puddle on the carpeting outside the door so that exposed second wire touches the wet carpeting and anyone attempting to open the door from the outside will be standing on the wet carpeting.
8. Insert the plug from the cord into an outlet, and ***do not touch the doorknob until you have unplugged the cord***.

HOW IT WORKS

Water conducts electricity. When someone grabs the doorknob from outside the door, the 110 volts of electricity from the wall socket surge through his body and his shoes touching the wet puddle on the carpeting to complete the circuit, giving the intruder a jolt of electricity.

WARNINGS

- Do not attempt to electrify the doorknob if the doorjamb is made from metal. Otherwise, you risk a short circuit, which may trip a circuit breaker or start a fire.
- Depending on the amperage traveling through the cord, the electric shock may kill the intruder, particularly if the person wears a pacemaker. *Electrifying a doorknob in a non-life-threatening situation could make you liable for premeditated murder or other serious charges.*

CULTURE SHOCK

- In the 1990 movie *Home Alone*, Kevin McCallister (Macaulay Culkin) places the loop of an electric charcoal lighter over the doorknob to the front door of his house. When con man Harry Lime (Joe Pesci) grabs the red-hot knob, he burns his hand.
- In a 1958 episode of the television series *Peter Gunn* (season 1, episode 11), private detective Gunn (Craig Stevens) escapes from his captors at the Olford Rest Home by cutting a cord from a lamp in his room and wiring it to the doorknob and the carpet in front of the door. He douses the carpet with water and calls for his jailer, who, upon stepping on the wet carpet, gets electrocuted.

4

CRUISE SHIPS AND STRANDED CRUISE SHIPS

The engine room of your luxury cruise ship catches fire and you're suddenly stranded for a week with 4,000 other people in the middle of the Gulf of Mexico—without air-conditioning, electricity, working toilets, running water, or sufficient food. What do you do first? Drag your mattress to the lido deck and pitch a tent using a bedsheet and claw hair clips? Or reach for the bottle of mouthwash you wisely filled with vodka, dyed green?

How to Sneak Liquor Aboard with Food Coloring

WHAT YOU NEED
- Utility knife
- Mouthwash bottle
- Funnel
- Hot water
- Vodka, gin, or white rum
- Food coloring

WHAT TO DO
1. Carefully and gently use the utility knife to cut around the circumference of the bottom of the cellophane seal surrounding the cap of the mouthwash bottle.
2. Unscrew the cap.
3. Pour the mouthwash into another bottle for home use.
4. Using a funnel, carefully fill the mouthwash bottle with hot water to rinse the bottle, swirl well, and empty—without wetting the labels on the bottle.
5. Fill the mouthwash bottle with vodka, gin, or white rum.
6. Add 3 drops of blue food coloring and 1 drop of green food coloring.
7. Replace the cap on the mouthwash bottle. Shake well to mix the coloring.
8. Place in your luggage near your toiletry kit or shampoos.

HOW IT WORKS
The plastic seal remains in place, making the mouthwash bottle look untouched. The food coloring does not spoil the quality of the alcohol or alter the taste.

HANDY RECIPES
- **Listerine Cool Mint (Blue):** 1 liter of vodka or gin, 3 drops of blue coloring, 1 drop of green coloring
- **Listerine (Green):** 1 liter of vodka or gin, 2 drops of green coloring
- **Listerine Original (Yellow):** 1 liter of vodka or gin, 2 drops of yellow coloring

- **Scope Classic Cool (Blue):** 1 liter of vodka or gin, 3 drops of blue coloring, 1 drop of green coloring
- **Scope Original Mint (Green):** 1 liter of vodka or gin, 2 drops of green coloring

HOLDING YOUR LIQUOR

- You can buy a flask disguised as a pair of binoculars, a bottle of sunscreen, a walking cane, a hairbrush, a camera, or a cell phone.
- Most cruise lines allow each passenger (21 years of age and older) to bring at least one bottle of wine or champagne aboard the ship on boarding day. If you wish to drink this bottle in the main dining room, there is generally a corkage fee for each bottle.
- If ship security catches you trying to bring prohibited alcohol or excessive quantities aboard the ship, they will generally seize those bottles and not return them (or, in some cases, store them for safekeeping until the end of the voyage).
- Be sure to read the alcohol policy for your cruise line before packing alcohol in your bags.

OFF THE BEATEN TRACK
How to Get Free Room Service

If you get hungry during your cruise but would rather stay in your stateroom, pick up the phone and order anything you wish from the room service menu. The food and delivery is complimentary during the daytime on all cruise lines and 24 hours a day on most, with the exception of Norwegian Cruise Line and Royal Caribbean, which charge a nominal fee per room service order delivered between midnight and 5:00 AM.

How to Hide Your Money in a Potato Chip Bag

WHAT YOU NEED
- Money
- Ziplock freezer bag
- Potato chip bag
- Chip clip

WHAT TO DO
1. Place your money inside the ziplock freezer bag.
2. Open the potato chip bag.
3. Insert the plastic bag of money into the bag of potato chips.
4. Arrange the potato chips so they are at the top of the bag, covering the plastic bag of money.
5. Fold down the top of the bag several times, and seal it shut with the chip clip.
6. Place the bag inconspicuously on a desktop or coffee table.

HOW IT WORKS
A potato chip bag appears commonplace, especially when sealed shut with a chip clip, but its humdrum veneer effectively disguises its clever utilitarian purpose.

WHEN THE CHIPS ARE DOWN
- On October 24, 2014, police in a suburb of St. Louis, Missouri, stopped 63-year-old Garry Russell Groves, of Fort Mitchell, Kentucky, for running a red light and having a headlight out on his car. With help from a police canine, officers found nearly a kilogram of cocaine hidden in a Lay's potato chip bag inside a duffel bag in the trunk.
- In 2011, US Homeland Security arrested 21-year-old Lemuel Giovani Espinosa of Compton, California, after Transportation Security Administration officers at Los Angeles International Airport discovered nearly five pounds of methamphetamine concealed inside potato chip bags in his backpack.
- In October 2010, officials at Rikers Island jail complex in New York placed rapper Lil Wayne in solitary confinement for a month as punishment for possession of contraband: headphones and a charger for a digital music player found hidden months earlier in a potato chip bag in a garbage can in the rapper's cell.

How to Prevent Seasickness with Ginger

WHAT YOU NEED

- ½ teaspoon of powdered ginger
- Glass of water
- Ginger teabags
- Ginger ale
- Ginger cookies

WHAT TO DO

1. To help prevent motion sickness, one hour before you commence your journey, mix a ½ teaspoon of powdered ginger in a glass of water.
2. Drink the tangy liquid.
3. During your cruise, drink cups of ginger tea or ginger ale, and snack on ginger cookies to quell the nausea that accompanies seasickness.

HOW IT WORKS

The gingerol and shogaol in ginger reduce intestinal contractions, neutralize indigestion, and prevent the brain from initiating the vomiting reflex. Ginger works best at *preventing* motion sickness rather than curing it. A study published in 1982 in the *Lancet* showed that ginger was more effective at relieving motion sickness than dimenhydrinate, the active ingredient in Dramamine. (Do not use ginger if you have gallstones. Ginger can increase bile production.)

GETTING YOUR SEA LEGS

- Scientists believe that seasickness is triggered when the brain receives sensory signals regarding motion that do not match. For instance, if you're reading a book on a lounge chair on a moving ship, your inner ear senses the motion of the ship but your eyes do not, making seasickness the likely result.
- Typically, the vestibular system—the organs of balance in the inner ear—accurately reports information about motion to the brain. However, unusual motions exceed the rate at which the vestibular system can relay information, causing the system to transmit false information that conflicts with information reported by the other senses. Scientists theorize that the brain presumes the vestibular system is providing

false information because the body has been poisoned. The brain reacts by triggering vomiting as a defense mechanism.

- Seasickness tends to subside after a day or so, once the traveler gets used to the motion and the brain grows accustomed to the contradictory input.
- Conventional drugs used to treat dizziness and the resulting nausea typically leave the patient feeling sedated.

OFF THE BEATEN TRACK
How to Avoid Seasickness

- **Avoid Alcohol.** To help prevent motion sickness, refrain from drinking any alcohol before or during your travels. Alcohol interferes with the communication between the eye, brain, and inner ear.
- **Dodge Triggers.** When you're feeling queasy, avoid smells that might trigger nausea, such as foods, engine fumes, or smoke.
- **Chew on Cloves.** If you're susceptible to seasickness, before boarding a boat chew on a few cloves. The eugenol in cloves helps stop the spasms. It can also prevent motion sickness if you chew it before traveling via train, airplane, or car.
- **Cruise at Night.** Traveling at night lessens the odds of seasickness by lessening the conflicting visual input. If you do get seasick, lying down and closing your eyes can lower the severity.
- **Look at the Horizon.** To prevent or reduce seasickness, minimize head movements and stare straight ahead at the distant horizon.
- **Press Proven Pressure Points.** To relieve feelings of nausea, identify the first crease on the inside of your wrist from the palm of your hand, measure two of your own thumb widths up your arm from the center of that crease, and press that point with your thumb firmly, until it hurts slightly, for 5 to 10 minutes. Repeat with your other wrist. Pressing this point on the wrist (known as the pericardium 6 point in acupuncture) can relieve nausea.
- **Sip Lemon Juice and Honey.** To calm your stomach, mix 3 tablespoons of lemon juice and 1 teaspoon of honey in an 8-ounce glass of warm water, and sip the warm drink as needed. ***Do not feed honey to infants under one year of age.*** Honey often carries a benign strain of *C. botulinum*, and an infant's immune system requires 12 months to develop before it can fight off disease.
- **Stop Reading.** To help avoid motion sickness, refrain from reading while traveling.

How to Keep Champagne Bubbly with Packaging Tape

WHAT YOU NEED
- Champagne bottle
- Clean washcloth
- Packaging tape

WHAT TO DO
1. To seal an open champagne bottle and keep the bubbly fresh, use a clean washcloth to wipe the mouth of the bottle to remove all moisture.
2. Adhere a small square of packaging tape flat over the mouth of the champagne bottle.
3. With your fingers, burnish the tape to the lip of the bottle to create a tight seal.
4. Place the sealed champagne bottle in a mini-refrigerator.
5. When you're ready to drink more champagne, simply remove the tape from the mouth of the bottle.

HOW IT WORKS
The packaging tape creates a tight seal over the mouth of the bottle like a substitute cork, preventing the carbonation from escaping from the bottle, keeping the champagne fresh.

BUBBLY
- If packaging tape is unavailable, cover the mouth of the champagne bottle with a piece of plastic wrap and secure it in place with a rubber band around the neck of the bottle.
- Starting in 1668, Benedictine monk Pierre Pérignon spent 47 years as winemaker at the Abbey Saint-Pierre of Hautvillers, near the town of Épernay, France, where he tried to prevent irritating bubbles from forming in the wine, which was a sign of poor wine making. He failed miserably. The bubbles in the wine resulted from the region's cold climate and short growing season. Farmers harvested grapes late in the year, due to necessity. When the grapes were pressed into grape

juice, the yeasts present on the grape skins did not have enough time to convert all the sugar in the juice into alcohol because the cold winter temperatures stopped the fermentation process. The winemakers bottled the wine, and when the spring arrived, the warm temperatures reawakened the fermentation process, which continued inside the sealed bottles. The refermentation produced carbon dioxide, which, trapped in the bottle, carbonated the wine, frequently causing the bottles to explode. To prevent the bottles from exploding, Dom Pérignon used stronger bottles developed by the English and sealed them closed with Spanish cork rather than the wood and oil-soaked hemp stoppers commonly used in his day. Although he failed to eliminate the bubbles, Dom Pérignon initiated and instituted the basic principles still used today to make champagne—and his sparkling white wine became the libation of choice by the English and French royalty and aristocracy.

How to Wash Your Clothes in the Swimming Pool

WHAT YOU NEED
- Bar of soap
- Bucket (or small garbage pail)

WHAT TO DO
1. Sitting alongside the pool, saturate the clothing items with pool water.
2. Rub the bar of soap into the clothes.
3. Knead the soap into the items for 3 minutes and pound the clothes against the edge of the pool.
4. Fill the bucket with pool water and pour it over the clothes to rinse the soap from them.
5. Repeat step 4 until all the soap has been rinsed from the clothing.
6. Wring the water from the garments.
7. Hang the garments to dry by draping the clothes over lounge chairs or bringing the clothes back to your cabin and draping them over the retractable clothesline in your shower.

HOW IT WORKS
The first 5 minutes of hand washing removes most of the dirt from the garments, and rinsing the garments in pool water removes the soapy lather from the clothes.

AIRING DIRTY LAUNDRY
Hundreds of men wash clothes in the Yamuna River, a tributary of the Ganges River in Delhi, India, turning one of the world's most polluted rivers into an enormous launderette. The men, known as *dhobis* (Hindi for "washermen"), visit homes to collect thousands of soiled garments before washing them in the river near the industrial neighborhood of Okhla, where the river overflows with sewage, industrial waste, and chemicals. They dry the clothes in bulk on the muddy banks.

How to Deodorize a Nonworking Toilet with Coffee

WHAT YOU NEED

- Scissors or knife
- Pair of panty hose
- Fresh coffee grounds

WHAT TO DO

1. To eliminate the smell of fecal matter from a bathroom with a broken toilet, use scissors or a knife to cut off one foot from a clean, used pair of panty hose.

2. Fill the panty hose foot with fresh coffee grounds, and tie a knot in the open end.

3. Tie the sachet to a towel bar or rack to hang over the toilet.

4. Shut the door and let it sit.

5. If you don't have a panty hose leg, fill a bowl or drinking glass with coffee grounds, and set the bowl or glass on the floor or countertop in the bathroom or wherever odors are giving you problems.

HOW IT WORKS

The coffee grounds absorb the foul odor.

How to Collect Rainwater with a Trash Can

WHAT YOU NEED

- Scissors or knife
- 2 plastic trash bags
- 4 deck chairs or outdoor lounge chairs
- Rope, string, dental floss, or claw hair clips
- Small stone (or small weight, like a few coins, a golf ball, or a metal spoon)
- Trash can
- Clean, empty bottles or other containers (such as soda cans, coffee mugs, or vases)

WHAT TO DO

1. Using the scissors or knife, slice open one of the trash bags along one side and the bottom to make one large plastic sheet. If you don't have a trash bag, use whatever material you have, such as a plastic shower curtain, a poncho, a space blanket, or a tarp.
2. In an open space outside, set up four deck chairs or outdoor lounge chairs in a square, as shown in the photo.
3. Using rope, string, dental floss, or claw hair clips, secure each corner of the plastic sheet to a different chair so that one side of the plastic sheet is positioned higher than its opposite side, creating a slope.

4. Place a small stone in the center of the plastic sheet to create a gutter so that the collected rainwater will flow toward the center of the plastic sheet and then down the middle of the lower side.

5. Line a trash can with the second plastic trash bag, and then place it under the lower side just beneath the gutter to collect the rainwater.

6. Have bottles or other containers ready to store or transport the water.

7. Filter and purify the water before drinking.

HOW IT WORKS

The suspended plastic sheet catches the rainwater, and the weight creates a gutter, diverting the flow of water. This simple device lets you capture more fresh water during a light rainfall and many gallons of fresh water in just a few minutes during a heavy rainfall.

RIGHT AS RAIN

- You can also collect rainwater from roofs and awnings. If the roof has a gutter, place a container underneath the downspout.

- Approximately 600 gallons of rainwater can be harvested from 1 inch of rain falling on a 1,000-square-foot roof.

- You can also capture fresh water during a rainstorm by setting out open containers, such as buckets, soda bottles with the tops cut off, cans, bowls, and pots. Use heavy objects to steady the containers and prevent the rocking of the boat from toppling over the containers.

- Filter debris from water by pouring the water through a plastic funnel lined with a coffee filter.

- To purify water at sea level, simply bring it to a rolling boil for 1 full minute.

- To purify water by adding liquid chlorine bleach, add 5 drops of household bleach (containing 5.25 to 8.25 percent chlorine) for each quart of water, mix thoroughly, and let the treated water stand for at least 60 minutes before drinking. For 1 gallon of water, add ¼ teaspoon of bleach.

How to Improvise a Tent from Bedsheets

WHAT YOU NEED

- Pocketknife
- Mattress
- Bedsheets
- Claw hair clips
- Safety pins (optional)

WHAT TO DO

1. To sleep outside on the deck, use a pocketknife to cut pieces of decorative rope from the cruise ship.
2. Drag your mattress to the deck.
3. Drape the sheets over anything that might serve as a frame—railings, chairs, or tables.
4. Use the claw hair clips and/ or pieces of decorative rope to hold the sheets to the frames.
5. If you need to use more than one bedsheet, connect the sheets together with safety pins.
6. Position your mattress under the tarp.

HOW IT WORKS

The frames hold the sheet aloft, and the sheet protects you from the harsh sun during the day and keeps you warmer beneath it at night.

SINK OR SWIM

In February 2013, when an engine fire crippled the Carnival *Triumph* cruise ship in the Gulf of Mexico, passengers spent some of their final hours drifting at sea by sleeping beneath makeshift canopies pitched from bedsheets, creating a tent city on the recreational decks.

OFF THE BEATEN TRACK

How to Cope with a Cruise Ship Crisis

- **Team Up.** Befriend other passengers for support and help to endure the ordeal together.
- **Ration Food.** Eat small, light meals, and if possible, set aside some of that food for snacks.
- **Stay Healthy.** If sanitation becomes unhygienic, use hand sanitizer and disinfecting wipes.
- **Skip the Alcohol.** While drinking may help you weather the trauma of being stranded at sea, alcohol causes dehydration and hinders you from reacting wisely to any emergency that may arise.
- **Organize Positive Activities.** To accent the positive, coordinate card games and other board games, create a Bible study group, or arrange other activities, such as enjoying the stars at night.
- **Set Up a Routine.** To ward off panic and gloom, take control of your time by scheduling time to walk the outdoor track, do calisthenics, or read a book.
- **Stay Hydrated.** Use sunscreen and drink plenty of water to avoid sunburn, dehydration, and heat stroke, which will only make a bad situation worse.
- **Avoid Negative People.** They'll suck the optimism out of you and fill you with despair. Instead, accentuate the positive, stop worrying, and savor the adventure.

How to Turn a Trash Can into a Toilet with a Pool Noodle

WHAT YOU NEED

- Scissors or utility knife
- Pool noodle
- Small circular trash can (or plastic 5-gallon paint bucket)
- Duct tape
- Plastic trash bag

WHAT TO DO

1. Using the scissors or utility knife, carefully cut the pool noodle to the length of the circumference of the mouth of the trash can.
2. Slice open the noodle lengthwise to create a slit that will fit over the lip of the trash can.
3. Hold the ends of the noodle together to form a ring with the slit facing down (perpendicular to the ring), and wrap a strip of duct tape around the ends to attach them together.
4. Cut a slit in the duct tape to match the slit in the noodle.
5. Line the trash can with a plastic trash bag, with the lip of the plastic bag folded back over the mouth of the trash can.
6. Fit the slit in the noodle over the edge of the mouth of the trash can or bucket.
7. To use the makeshift toilet, sit on the noodle ring.
8. When you finish doing your business, remove the noodle ring, carefully remove the plastic trash bag, seal it securely, and discard it appropriately.

HOW IT WORKS

The bendable polyethylene noodle ring provides a somewhat comfortable toilet seat.

NOODLING AROUND

Two Canadians from Ontario, Steve Hartman and Rick Koster, insist they independently invented the pool noodle—a polyethylene foam tube for playing or floating in swimming pools. In 1980, Hartman founded

Industrial Thermo Polymers (ITP) with his father and started making backer rods, foam tubing used in expansion joints in buildings and road-ways. Someone threw one of the rods in the family swimming pool, and Hartman soon realized he had a successful toy on his hands. He began marketing colored foam pool noodles. Meanwhile, Koster, inspired by his kids, who swam competitively, began experimenting with floating toys. In 1986, Koster, having devised a number of floating noodles, attempted to market the Water Woggle, a white foam tube with a foam serpent head. He quickly dropped the serpent head and settled on a cylindrical foam tube.

In 1990 Koster asked ITP to mass-produce his Water Woggles. The collaboration lasted several months but ultimately fell apart. Hartman claims that Koster walked away from the arrangement when he found out ITP was already selling pool noodles. Koster insists that Hartman stole his idea. Koster sued Hartman but eventually dropped the lawsuit because he couldn't afford the legal fees. Neither Koster nor Hartman patented the invention, so now anyone can manufacture the pool toy.

EVERY TRICK IN THE BOOK
Using Your Noodle

You can make a wide variety of objects from pool noodles:

- **Boot Trees.** Cut the noodle to two lengths the height of your boots. Insert in the boots to keep them standing tall.
- **Christmas Wreath.** Duct tape the noodle into a loop, cover with burlap, and decorate.
- **Door Stopper.** Prevent kids from slamming the door shut by cutting open a noodle lengthwise and placing it over the edge of the door.
- **Extension Cord Storage.** Slice open a noodle lengthwise and store extension cords neatly inside.
- **Floating Beer Cooler.** Cut a noodle into four pieces the length of each side of a large plastic container, run a rope through the noodle pieces, and tie them securely under the lip of the container.
- **Indoor Basketball Hoop.** Duct tape the ends together, duct tape one end of the hoop to the wall, and use an inflatable beach ball as the basketball.
- **Marble Racetrack.** Cut a noodle in half lengthwise to create a marble racetrack that keeps the kids occupied for hours.
- **Napkin Rings.** Cut slices from a pool noodle and insert a napkin through each ring.
- **Rake Storage.** Cut a noodle the length of the head of a rake, slice open the noodle lengthwise, and store the prongs of the rake inside to prevent accidents.
- **Trampoline Spring Protectors.** Cover your trampoline springs with pool noodles.

How to Make a Life Vest from Bleach Jugs

WHAT YOU NEED

- 4 clean, empty bleach jugs
- Rope, 3-foot length (or belt)

WHAT TO DO

1. Secure the caps in place on the bleach jugs.
2. Knot a piece of rope around the handles of the bleach jugs (or slip the belt through the handles with the handles facing inward toward your body).
3. Tie the ends of the rope together to form a loop, which can then fit around your waist or chest. If using a belt, simply wear the belt.
4. ***Enter the water slowly*** to prevent the jugs from causing you injury. (If you can only enter the water by jumping, do not tie the ends of the rope around your waist or chest until you are in the water.)

HOW IT WORKS

Once you are in the water with the life vest around your body, the water displacement created by the air in the jugs will keep you afloat.

STAYING AFLOAT

In a dire emergency, you can improvise a float from:

- **Bucket.** Turned upside down and submerged to trap air inside.
- **Condoms.** Inflate and tie knots in two condoms, tie a shoelace to the knot in each condom, and position to wear the shoelace around your back and under your arms.
- **Ice Chest (or Cooler).** Sealed shut with duct tape, if necessary.
- **Plastic Trash Bag.** Filled with air and knotted (or twist tied) shut.
- **Large Plastic Salad Bowl.** Turned upside down and submerged to trap air inside.

How to Desalinate and Purify Ocean Water with a T-Shirt

WHAT YOU NEED

- Clean, empty coffee can (or a clean, empty, wide-mouthed vase)
- Small trash can (or bucket)
- Clean T-shirt
- Plastic wrap
- A small stone or other small weight (such as a few coins, a golf ball, or metal keys)

WHAT TO DO

1. Stand the coffee can in the center of the trash can.
2. Saturate the T-shirt with seawater (or saltwater from the cruise ship's swimming pool), and place it on the floor of the bucket, wrapped around the coffee can—without getting any saltwater inside the can.
3. Stretch a sheet of plastic wrap over the mouth of the bucket, making it taut, and airtight around the rim of the bucket.
4. Place a small stone or other small weight in the center of the sheet of plastic wrap so the sheet dips like a cone with its vertex pointing directly over the center of the coffee can or vase.
5. Set the bucket in direct sunlight for several hours.

HOW IT WORKS

The heat from the sun causes the seawater to evaporate, leaving the salt particles in the cloth at the bottom of the bucket. The evaporated water condenses on the underside of the plastic wrap, and then that freshwater drips into the can.

TAKE IT WITH A GRAIN OF SALT

- Humans can safely drink water that contains less that 0.5 percent salt. Seawater contains approximately 3.5 percent salt.
- A person who drinks only seawater will die of thirst. The kidneys cannot filter out all the salt. To eliminate the excess salt taken in by drinking seawater, the kidneys force you to urinate more water than you drank. For every quart of saltwater you drink, your body produces a quart

and a half of urine, according to Elmhurst College, causing you to die from dehydration.

- As of 2009, more than 1,400 desalination plants were operating in the world, producing more than 15 billion gallons of water daily.
- The world's largest reverse osmosis desalination plant, opened in 2010, is located in Hadera, Israel.
- The Western Hemisphere's largest desalination plant, being built in Carlsbad, California, by an Israeli company in cooperation with a local development company, will produce an estimated 50 million gallons of drinking water every day.

OFF THE BEATEN TRACK
Get the Best Cabin for the Least Money

Before you choose a cabin aboard any cruise ship, study the floor plans of the ship to make sure you know everything possible about your accommodations.

- Small inside cabins located in the bowels of the ship are the least expensive, while large outside cabins with a balcony on the upper decks are the most expensive. Remember, unless you're on your honeymoon, you'll be spending very little time in your cabin, and regardless of the price of your cabin, you get to experience the same shows, meals, and activities.
- To avoid seasickness, book a cabin in the center of the ship on the lowest possible deck. The cabin will rock and seesaw far less than cabins on upper decks and those toward the front or rear of the ship.
- If you seek a quiet room, avoid cabins under the casino, a pool deck, a dance floor, a basketball court, the gym, the running track, or the children's activity centers. Also, steer clear of a cabin near a stairwell, elevator bank, the vibrations of the engine room, or housekeeping maintenance closets.
- Book early. The less expensive cabins tend to sell out first.
- Most cabins have twin lower beds, which can usually be pushed together by the steward to make a queen-size bed. Many cabins with two twin beds are equipped with two more berths, usually upper bunks (which pull down from the wall or ceiling). A single passenger who prefers not to share a cabin generally pays a supplemental fee.
- If you want a cabin with a balcony, note that cabins in the very back of the ship tend to have the largest balconies.

5

TRAINS AND BUSES

"Enclosing every thin man, there's a fat man demanding elbow-room," wrote British novelist Evelyn Waugh in *Officers and Gentlemen*. Riding a train or bus can be simultaneously exhilarating and exasperating. The sense of freedom, the feeling of adventure, and the beauty of the bucolic scenery clash with the hassles of guarding your luggage, sleeping upright in a chair, maintaining your hygiene, enduring ennui, dealing with inconsiderate passengers, and coping with the foul stench of the restroom. Do you sit back and enjoy the ride? Or worry yourself sick?

How to Shower on a Train with a Water Bottle

WHAT YOU NEED

- 1-liter water bottle
- Restroom sink
- Boiling-hot water (optional)
- Washcloth
- Soap
- Shampoo
- Towel

WHAT TO DO

1. Carefully fill the water bottle halfway with hot water from the tap in the restroom, or, if the water is not hot enough, with boiling-hot water from the café or dining car.

2. Fill the rest of the bottle with cold water from the tap in the restroom.

3. Seal the cap or lid of the bottle shut securely, and shake well to yield lukewarm water.

4. Saturate the washcloth with water, and rub yourself with the damp cloth. Rinse the washcloth frequently, using no more than half the water in the bottle.

5. Use the soap to lather yourself, but minimize the amount you use. Lathering up excessively requires more water than you have to effectively wash off the suds. Do use soap for your underarms and private parts, and wash off the suds with the damp washcloth.

6. Use a drop of shampoo to lather up your hair. You'll be surprised how little shampoo you need to accomplish this. Bending over to hold your head down near the sink, use the remaining water to rinse your hair clean.

7. Towel yourself dry.

HOW IT WORKS

The most convenient way to use a basin for bathing is to use cloths or sponges to bring up the water to the rest of the body, while standing or kneeling, and then using a pitcher to rinse off soap and dirt. When water is in short supply or a shower or bathtub is unavailable, a sponge bath cleans the body, though less effectively than a shower or bath.

SQUEAKY CLEAN

- To give yourself a refreshing sponge bath, fill a sink with tepid water and add two tablespoons of baking soda. Dampen a sponge or washcloth in the solution and wipe yourself down. The baking soda, a natural deodorizer, leaves you smelling fresh.
- A sponge bath, an alternative to bathing in a tub or showering, is commonly used for hospital patients who cannot stand in a shower or bathe safely in a tub, young babies who could slip in a tub, and patients with dementia or Alzheimer's disease who may become disoriented or violent.

OFF THE BEATEN TRACK
How to Get the Best Seat on a Train or Bus

The most comfortable place to sit on a train or bus is undoubtedly on the inside. Here are more practical tips:

TRAINS

- On a single-level train, the most comfortable seats are in the middle of the car. These seats are farthest away from the doors (which passengers repeatedly open, allowing noise from outside to enter, and then slam shut again) and the wheels (giving you a smoother ride).
- On the upper level of a Superliner, sit ahead of the stairs (because the light is on all night) but not too near the backdoor.
- For more legroom on a Superliner, sit just behind the stairs on the upper level.
- For a smoother ride on a Superliner, sit in the center on the lower level. The corridor to other cars is located on the upper level, minimizing foot traffic on the lower level. However, the clickety-clack of track noise is less prominent on the upper level.
- For the best side of the train for the most scenic views, ask the conductor or consider where the train travels on a map. For instance, on a trip from San Francisco to Los Angeles, traveling along the coastline, the right side will afford the best views. On the return trip heading north, the left side will be the most picturesque.
- Before you settle into your seat, make sure the overhead lights, reclining mechanism, tray table, and footrest work properly.
- If you're seeking a peaceful journey free from people talking on cell phones, playing loud video games, or yakking at high volume, choose a seat in the quiet car.

BUSES

- The most comfortable seats are in the middle of the bus, farthest away from the wheels (giving you a smoother ride).
- Avoid sitting anywhere near the restroom in the rear of the bus. Otherwise you'll be bombarded with the unpleasant aroma of industrial-strength cleansers and human waste.
- Before you settle into your seat, make sure the overhead lights, reclining mechanism, tray table, and footrest work properly.
- When you first take a seat, sit in an aisle seat, so boarding passengers are less likely to sit next to you—if you wish to be left alone. No one wants to squeeze past a stranger for a window seat, improving your chances of getting two seats to yourself.
- If the bus provides television screens with free videos, select a seat with a direct view of the screen.
- Determine where the sun will be positioned during your journey. To avoid the blinding light or blazing heat, sit on the left side of the bus if you are headed north in the morning and on the right side in the afternoon.

TRICKS OF THE TRADE

To keep a row of two seats on a train or bus to yourself . . .

- Sit in the aisle seat and pile your bags (daypack, purse, briefcase, shopping bags) on the seat next to you to dissuade others from sitting next to you or asking you to move your belongings.
- Avoid making eye contact with anyone boarding the train or bus, or close your eyes and pretend to be asleep.
- Put on a pair of headphones, bob your head, and quietly sing to the music. Most people will avoid sitting next to anyone talking to himself or acting potentially crazy.

How to Bathe with Baby Wipes

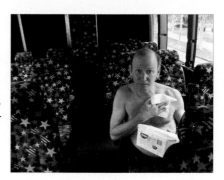

WHAT YOU NEED
- Baby wipes in unscented, aloe, or "fresh scent" (avoid floral or baby powder scents)
- Deodorant

WHAT TO DO
1. Lock yourself in a private bathroom aboard the train or bus or find a securely locked bathroom stall in a bus station.
2. Remove your clothing.
3. Wipe down your body thoroughly, using three to four baby wipes.
4. Repeat if necessary.
5. Apply deodorant liberally.

HOW IT WORKS
The plastic container baby wipes come in keeps the towelettes moist, and the wipes clean grime and perspiration from your body.

CLEAN UP YOUR ACT
- Do not bathe with baby wipes more than twice in a row without a genuine shower. Otherwise you will begin to reek.
- In 2009, *People* reported that Brad Pitt sometimes cleans up with baby wipes to save time between scene changes on the set.
- *Mother Jones* reported in 2010 that although showers comprise 17 percent of indoor residential water use in the United States, bathing with baby wipes is not environmentally sound. The water required to grow the wood, manufacture the paper, produce the chemical solution the wipes are soaked in, and package and ship the wipes far exceeds the water used for a five-minute shower with a low-flow showerhead.
- Wipes may be a better choice than showers during droughts or disasters with limited water supply, conceded Jonathan Kaledin, a water conservation expert at the Nature Conservancy, but a short shower is generally more environmentally efficient than bathing with wipes.
- To bathe efficiently: lower the temperature on your water heater to save energy, turn the water off while you soap up, and install a low-flow showerhead.

EVERY TRICK IN THE BOOK

Other Uses for Baby Wipes

Baby wipes have a wide array of alternative uses:

- **Coffee Stain Remover.** Blot up spilled coffee from a rug or carpet. Baby wipes absorb coffee without leaving a stain.
- **Hand Cleaner.** Keep a box of baby wipes in the trunk of your car to clean your hands after pumping gas or changing the oil.
- **Scrape and Bruise Sanitizer.** Baby wipes are great for cleaning a minor abrasion.
- **Shoe Shiner.** Simply wipe your shoes with a baby wipe.
- **Toilet Paper Substitute.** Use baby wipes as gentle toilet paper to avoid aggravating sensitive hemorrhoids or after an episiotomy.

How to Secure Your Luggage with a Shoelace

WHAT YOU NEED
- Shoelace (or necktie or belt)

WHAT TO DO

1. When traveling on a train or bus, turn your luggage in the luggage rack so the handles face away from the aisle.
2. Use a shoelace to tie your suitcases together and, if possible, to the railing on the rack—all with secure double knots.

HOW IT WORKS
Turning the handles away from the aisle makes the bags harder to grab quickly without creating a scene. Tying the two bags together prevents a thief from grabbing one bag without being tethered by the second bag. Fastening the bags to the railing also prevents the bags from leaving the luggage rack.

A MIXED BAG
- Thieves are more apt to steal smaller items than a large, bulky suitcase that inhibits a fast getaway.
- An opportunistic thief will, in all likelihood, choose the easiest target—which a bag locked to a railing is not.
- Carry a lightweight, retractable cable lock (available wherever bicycle accessories are sold), or make your own cable with parts at a hardware store and purchase a combination lock. Use the cable to tie your suitcases together and lock them around a steel pole or rail on the luggage rack.
- Trains stop in stations for short times, so if you lock your luggage, be sure to leave sufficient time before your stop to unfasten the lock and chain.
- A lock and cable can also be used to strap your luggage together when being held by the concierge, to a fixture in a hotel room, or inside the trunk of your car.
- If you're traveling by bus with your bags in the luggage compartment, keep watch when the bus stops to make sure none of your luggage walks off by itself.

RUNAWAY TRAINS

Scores of Hollywood movies and television shows depict runaway trains and actors cleverly stopping them. And the winners are:

- **Death Train** (2003). Escaped convicts commandeer a passenger train in the Mexican countryside and hold the passengers hostage at gunpoint while the runaway train hurtles toward a deadly impact.
- **How the West Was Won** (1962). The film climaxes with a gunfight between Zeb Rawlings (George Peppard) and Charlie Gant (Eli Wallach) aboard a runaway train hurtling across the desert.
- **Mystery Train** (1931). During a jewel heist on the *Transcontinental Limited*, a group of passengers gets trapped in a runaway Pullman car hurtling down a steep mountain grade.
- **Runaway Train** (1985). Jon Voight and Eric Roberts star as escaped prisoners trapped on a runaway train in Alaska.
- **Silver Streak** (1976). Gene Wilder and Richard Pryor try to prevent a passenger train from colliding with a train station.
- **The Taking of Pelham One Two Three** (1974). Hijackers override a New York City subway car's dead-man switch, causing the runaway train to travel faster and faster toward the end of the line.
- **Unstoppable** (2010). Denzel Washington tries to stop a runaway train loaded with toxic chemicals and headed for a small town in the Midwest.

How to Make a Portable Television with a Ziplock Bag

WHAT YOU NEED

- Smart phone
- Ziplock freezer bag
- Ballpoint pen
- Headset
- Binder clip (optional)

WHAT TO DO

1. Place your smart phone inside the ziplock freezer bag.
2. Zip the bag shut most of the way (leaving an opening roughly 1 inch long), suck the remaining air from the bag, and seal the bag shut.
3. Use the tip of a ballpoint pen to punch a hang hole in the top of the bag, in the center just above the zipper strip.
4. Poke a small hole in the side of the plastic bag to accommodate your headset plug.
5. Hang the bag from the latch used to hold the tray table upright.
6. If desired, secure the bag to the latch with a binder clip.

HOW IT WORKS

The latch holds the plastic bag in place, and the bag serves as a hammock for your smart phone.

SCREEN TIME

- Placing a cell phone inside a securely sealed ziplock bag prevents the device from getting wet from rain or perspiration or when sitting near a pool, sailing in open waters, visiting the beach, or fishing.
- A plastic bag is a selectively permeable membrane, meaning some molecules can diffuse through the plastic. Through osmosis, a solvent (such as water) with a low concentration of solute outside the plastic bag can move through the plastic into a high concentration of solute inside the bag.
- In an episode of the television show *The League* ("The Sacko Bowl," season 2, episode 13), Jenny (Katie Aselton) pulls back the shower curtain to find Kevin (Stephen Rannazzisi) holding a smart phone in a plastic bag.

EVERY TRICK IN THE BOOK
Putting the Zip in Ziplock

- **Bathing Suit Bag.** Store a wet swimsuit in a large ziplock freezer bag until you can let it dry out properly, to avoid getting everything in your bag wet and containing the possible growth of mold or mildew.
- **Camera and mp3 Player Bags.** Store your camera and mp3 player in a ziplock bag to keep your electronic devices dry.
- **Camera Protector.** To protect your camera from rain, place the camera inside a large, upside-down ziplock freezer bag and cut a tight hole for the lens to stick through. Use a rubber band to secure the plastic bag to the end of the lens. Insert your hand into the upside-down bag to use the camera.
- **Coffee and Tea Kit.** Store tea bags and packets of instant coffee, sugar, and creamer so you're always prepared for a coffee or tea break.
- **Electronic Cord Storage.** Wires and chargers easily fit in a ziplock bag.
- **Fish Food Holder.** When snorkeling, feed the fish with a few slices of bread stored in a ziplock bag.
- **Instant Ice Pack.** If you need an ice pack, simply fill the bag at the hotel ice machine and wrap it in a thin towel.
- **Jewelry Box.** Place your rings, earrings, and necklaces in a ziplock bag to prevent them from getting scattered or misplaced.
- **Miniature Travel Hamper.** Place your dirty laundry in a ziplock bag to prevent any soiled garments from contaminating clean clothes.
- **Portable Medicine Cabinet.** Store your bottles of prescription and over-the-counter medicines and vitamins in a large ziplock bag.
- **Store Important Papers.** Place passports, travel documents, money, and souvenir brochures inside a waterproof ziplock bag.
- **Toiletry Bag.** Place all your liquid and gel toiletries from your carry-on luggage in a ziplock bag before going through an airport security check to hasten the inspection.

How to Endure Foul Restroom Odors with Vicks VapoRub

WHAT YOU NEED
- Jar of Vicks VapoRub
- Tissue (or a few sheets of toilet paper)

WHAT TO DO
1. Before using a foul-smelling restroom, smear a dab of Vicks VapoRub above your upper lip.
2. Be sure to place the jar in a safe place before using the restroom so it doesn't accidentally drop into the toilet or onto the floor.
3. When you're finished using the toilet, wipe the pungent salve from your face with a tissue.

HOW IT WORKS
A dab of Vick VapoRub—a salve made from eucalyptus and menthol—masks the scent of foul-smelling odors.

DOWN THE TUBES
- On trains in many parts of the world, human waste is flushed onto the train tracks, and signs warn against using the toilets while the train is stopped in a station.
- On a bus, waste is held in a holding tank directly beneath the toilet. In some bus toilets a flap closes to hide the view of the holding tank. Other bus toilets have no flap, leaving the holding tank in view. Bus toilets use a blue formaldehyde product to help mask the odor. A vent in the bathroom pulls odors from the bathroom to outside the bus. Bus operators usually empty the holding tank through a sewer hose and into a sewer after every trip to minimize odors.
- In the first edition of *Tibet: A Travel Survival Kit* (Lonely Planet, 1986), authors Michael Buckley and Robert Strauss provide a memorable description of the toilets in Tibet: "The trek to the toilet is an arduous one and you'd best come well-equipped for the ordeal. First, try not to look at the floor. Some of these toilets look like they've been backed up since the 1st century. Since the sanitation system is nonexistent, the stuff just stays in the fly-infested pits below. A nose-peg and a set

of horse-halters would be a good idea. A swig of whisky before the assault is recommended, and some are known to put a dab of Tiger Balm or Chanel No. 5 on the upper lip to minimize the overpowering smells. Toilet paper is mandatory—carry your own supply. You'll need a flashlight to make sure you don't fall into the back-up at night."

- People working in a morgue often smear Vicks VapoRub above their upper lip to mask the odor of a decomposing corpse—as dramatized in the 1991 movie *The Silence of the Lambs*.

- In 2007, zookeepers at Paultons Park near Romsey in Hampshire, England, prevented their two existing meerkats from instinctually attacking three newcomers by putting Vicks VapoRub on the nose of each meerkat to hide the scents of the others long enough for all of them to accept each other.

- In 1905, Lunsford Richardson, a pharmacist working in his brother-in-law's drugstore in Selma, North Carolina, aspired to create an ointment to decongest sinuses and relieve chest congestion. In the backroom laboratory of the pharmacy, he blended menthol (a newly introduced extract from oil of peppermint), petroleum jelly, and other ingredients and named his creation Richardson's Croup and Pneumonia Cure Salve. When rubbed on the forehead and chest, the salve—vaporized by body heat—stimulated blood circulation and decongested blocked sinuses. Demand for the salve exceeded Richardson's wildest expectations, prompting the pharmacist to market his new remedy. Seeking a catchier name for the product, Richardson decided to name it in honor of his brother-in-law, Joshua Vick. He advertised Vicks VapoRub in local newspapers, with coupons redeemable for a free trial jar.

OFF THE BEATEN TRACK
Long-Distance Survival Secrets

- **Bring Snacks.** A few treats (fruit, granola bars, mixed nuts, sandwiches, and beverages) provide sustenance to help you endure the long haul and help save money at restaurant stops.
- **Watch Your Bags.** If you check any luggage, wait to see that it gets loaded into the compartment on the side of the bus. Also, make sure the destination tags on your checked luggage match your ticket destination.
- **Use the Restroom at Rest Stops.** Rather than using the not-so-sanitary bathroom in the back of the bus and getting your bum splashed with blue disinfectant, take advantage of rest stops at bus stations with more hygienic facilities.
- **Bring a Neck Pillow, Sleep Mask, and Earplugs.** To make yourself more comfortable and help you sleep, pack these luxury items. In a pinch, a rolled-up jacket or sweatshirt doubles as a pillow.
- **Bring Entertainment.** A book, iPod, laptop computer, or portable DVD player will help pass the time. If the bus line provides free Wi-Fi, enjoy use of the Internet.
- **Do Not Bring Drugs or Alcohol.** The driver has the power to throw drunk passengers off the bus, or call the police to have drug users escorted off the bus and arrested.
- **Keep Your Valuables Concealed on Your Person.** Prevent your wallet, purse, or other valuables from getting stolen by keeping them close to your body.
- **Travel Light.** Take a small wheeled suitcase and a small carry-on bag to avoid having to lug large suitcases through a bus station.
- **Bring Toilet Paper and Hand Sanitizer.** This way, you're prepared for an odious bus toilet.
- **Stretch.** When the bus makes a rest stop, get off to stretch your legs, which will help rejuvenate your weary mind and body.
- **Return to the Bus in Time.** If you get off the bus at a rest stop, make sure to take your valuables with you and get back on the bus in plenty of time. Bus drivers abandon stragglers at rest stops.

How to Jump from a Moving Train with a Suitcase of Clothes

WHAT YOU NEED

- Rugged clothing
- Extra clothes
- Blankets
- Pillows
- Towels
- Newspaper
- Pocketknife (optional)

WHAT TO DO

1. Prepare yourself for the reality of the situation. If you jump from a train moving at 70 miles per hour, inertia will cause you to go flying into the air at the same velocity as the train. In other words, you'll hit the ground while moving forward at roughly 70 miles per hour. The only thing to stop your forward velocity is the friction between your body and the ground, which can cause serious injuries or death. Realize that if you survive the initial impact and subsequent rolling, your injuries will doubtlessly require hospitalization.

2. If, after considering the likely consequences, you still wish to jump, put on rugged clothing and stuff other garments, blankets, pillows, towels, or crumpled-up sheets of newspaper into your clothes for padding. Also secure padding around your head, knees, hips, and joints. If necessary and possible, use a pocketknife to slash open the seat cushions and use the foam padding.

3. Walk to the back of the train, or locate a door between adjoining carriages that you can force open.

4. Wait for the train to slow while moving uphill or rounding a bend, and choose to jump when the train passes a grassy area without literal stumbling blocks like trees, shrubs, fences, walls, pavement, boulders, rocks, or gravel.

5. Hurl your suitcase from the train.

6. Squat close to the floor or the bottom step, bend your knees, and spring forward, leaping perpendicular to the direction of the train and as far as possible from the moving train.

7. Do not attempt to land on your feet, which risks breaking your ankles or legs. Instead, use your hands and arms to cover your head, straighten your body, allow your entire body to hit the ground at once, and then roll like a log.

HOW IT WORKS

Layers of clothing and padding will help protect your body from injury when you hit the ground at 70 miles per hour. Jumping perpendicular to the direction of the train prevents your forward momentum from hurtling you toward the steel wheels and tracks. Allowing the length of your body to hit the ground at once disperses the impact, and rolling on the ground may further help mitigate physical injury.

6

CARS

"I forgot where I parked the car." "The battery's dead." "The car's stuck in the snow." "I have to go to the bathroom." "Oops, I locked the keys in the car." "The windshield is covered with dead bugs."

For every dumb problem, there's an ingenious solution. You can locate your car with a water bottle, recharge a dead car battery with red wine, create traction with kitty litter, use a Gatorade bottle for a toilet, and easily break into a locked car with a clothes hanger. All you need is the know-how. And the courage to spray your hood with cooking spray before starting your trip and to wipe it clean with a pair of panty hose afterward.

How to Remove Dead Insects from the Windshield and Hood with Panty Hose

WHAT YOU NEED

- Dishwashing liquid
- Bucket
- Water
- Pair of panty hose

WHAT TO DO

1. Add a few drops of dishwashing liquid to a bucket, and fill it with water.
2. Ball up a pair of clean, used panty hose, and dampen it with the soapy water.
3. Use the nylon garment to gently scrub dead insects from the hood of the car.

HOW IT WORKS

The nylon is a mild abrasive that cleans off the bugs without scratching the finish.

EVERY TRICK IN THE BOOK
Bugz n the Hood

- **Baby Shampoo.** Add a few drops of baby shampoo to a bucket of warm water, dampen a sponge in the solution, and rub the car to remove insects easily and effortlessly.
- **Baking Soda.** To clean dead insects from the hood and windshield of a car or truck, sprinkle baking soda on a damp sponge, wipe down the hood or windshield, and then wipe it clean with a dry cloth. The baking soda is a mild abrasive that removes insects without harming the finish of the car.
- **Dryer Sheet.** To clean lovebugs from the hood and windshield of a car or truck, wet the vehicle and then rub the dead insects with a wet dryer sheet. The antistatic elements in the mildly abrasive sheet make cleaning off the lovebugs effortless.
- **Soda.** To clean insects off a car windshield, pour a can or bottle of carbonated soda over the windshield and squeegee clean.

How to Clean Cloudy Headlights with Toothpaste

WHAT YOU NEED
- Toothpaste, regular white (not gel)
- Sponge (or rag)
- Water
- Clean, soft cloth (or paper towels)

WHAT TO DO
1. Place a small amount of toothpaste on a sponge.
2. Rub the toothpaste onto the headlights in small circular motions for a few minutes.
3. Rinse clean with water and a clean, soft cloth.

HOW IT WORKS
Ultraviolet radiation from the sun degrades polycarbonate plastic, creating an oxidized haze—similar to plaque on your teeth—on the transparent headlight covers, turning them increasingly opaque. Airborne flecks also scratch and chip the plastic headlight covers. Toothpaste is a mild abrasive that cleans the plastic without scratching it. The cleansing lasts roughly three months, depending on how much you drive.

SEEING THE LIGHT
- Use only regular toothpaste to clean headlights. Tartar-control or whitening toothpastes can damage the plastic.
- To make your clean headlights shine, apply some car wax to the plastic cover, let dry, and buff with a clean cloth.
- For a more durable fix, mask the area around the headlights with blue painter's tape or electrical tape. Use wet 400-grit sandpaper to remove the factory coating and outer layer of haze, and wet 1200-grit and 1500-grit sandpaper to smooth any scratches. Apply a fine polishing compound, followed by a UV sealant.
- Dirty headlights can significantly dim the brightness of the light and diminish your visibility, increasing your risk of accidents.

How to Improvise an Air Bag with a Beach Ball

WHAT YOU NEED
- Inflatable beach ball, 20-inch diameter

WHAT TO DO
1. If the vehicle is not equipped with a working air bag for the passenger seats, inflate the beach ball and hold it in your lap, grasping it on either side.
2. If you anticipate an accident, quickly raise the ball in front of your face.

HOW IT WORKS
The driver's air bag is roughly the size of a large, fully inflated beach ball. The passenger's air bag can be much larger to make up for the space filled by the steering wheel. If the vehicle you're riding in doesn't have a functioning air bag, holding a beach ball in front of your face can offer *some* protection from injury during a crash by cushioning you during impact and protecting your body from hitting any objects inside the car.

FLOATING ON AIR
- A real air bag is connected to a crash sensor, which will deploy the bag if the car gets into a head-on and near-head-on crash at 8 to 14 miles per hour or greater.
- The crash sensor triggers an igniter to produce a gas, typically nitrogen or argon, to fill the air bag and deploy it in approximately 0.05 seconds. The air bag deflates almost immediately.
- The crash sensor may malfunction and deploy the air bag at the wrong time, too late, or not at all—resulting in a serious injury or death.
- A deploying air bag can cause abrasions or burns (from its speed), an asthma attack (from the chemicals released), or a severe eye injury (from its impact).
- If the driver or passenger is sitting too close to the air bag, the force of a deploying air bag can cause death.

How to Fashion a Portable Toilet from a Gatorade Bottle

WHAT YOU NEED

- Clean, empty Gatorade bottle with cap
- Toilet paper (or tissue)
- Duct tape
- Hand sanitizer (or baby wipes)

WHAT TO DO

1. If you're the driver, pull over to a secluded spot on the side of the road. If you're a passenger and the driver doesn't wish to pull over, cover your torso with a blanket or towel for privacy.
2. If you're male, unzip your fly. If you're female, either pull down your pants or lift up your skirt and lower your underwear.
3. Carefully urinate into the bottle. If you're female, position the mouth of the bottle as close as possible to your urethra, creating a tight seal against the mouth of the bottle. Keep toilet paper in hand to blot up any accidental seepage.
4. Cap the bottle securely.
5. Adhere a strip of duct tape to the bottle so no one will mistake it for a beverage.
6. Store the bottle upright to avoid spills or leaks.
7. Wash your hands with hand sanitizer, baby wipes, or soap and water.
8. When you reach a restroom, pour the urine into a urinal or toilet, and discard the bottle in a garbage can. Or rinse the bottle with soap and water for reuse solely as a portable urinal.

HOW IT WORKS

The wide mouth of the bottle provides ample room to urinate into it without creating a mess. The screw-top lid secures the liquid safely inside, averting spills or leaks.

HITTING THE BOTTLE

- Several companies manufacture and sell portable urinal bottles designed for both men and women, equipped with an adapter to accommodate the female anatomy. The bottle can be used for camping or travel.

- The military uses plastic urine containers as tent toilets.
- In Richard Wagamese's novel *Ragged Company*, Digger remembers, "No one said nothin' when I couldn't walk to the bathroom an' had to piss in an empty bottle at night."

OFF THE BEATEN TRACK
How to Save at the Pump

- **Shop Around for the Lowest Gas Prices.** To find the nearest and most inexpensive gas station, preview prices online at GasBuddy.com or GasPriceWatch.com. Or use the apps GasBuddy or GasBook.
- **Fill 'er Up Before the Gas Level Drops Below a Quarter of a Tank.** Driving around with too little gas in the tank can cause the fuel pump to burn out, necessitating a costly repair.
- **Secure the Gas Cap Closed.** After filling the tank with gas, twist the gas cap until it clicks three times. With older vehicles, make certain the gas cap is tightly in place. A poorly fitting or missing gas cap can lessen a vehicles mileage up to 10 percent.
- **Get a Credit Card That Cuts Gasoline Costs.** Several credit cards, including cards issued by gas station chains, offer up to 5 percent cash back on gasoline purchases. Discover the options online at www.cardhub.com or www.cardratings.com.

How to Create Emergency Traction with Kitty Litter

WHAT YOU NEED
- Clean, empty coffee cans
- Kitty litter
- Duct tape

WHAT TO DO
1. Fill clean, empty coffee cans with unused kitty litter and cap them securely with the lids.
2. Adhere a strip of duct tape over each lid to secure it in place.
3. Store the cans of kitty litter in your trunk.
4. If your tires get stuck in snow or ice, clear any snow away from the tailpipe. Otherwise, a blocked tailpipe will send deadly carbon monoxide gas inside the car.
5. Dig away as much excess snow and ice from in front of the tires as possible.
6. Turn the steering wheel to straighten the front wheels (provided no objects obstruct the path of the car).
7. Grab the prepared cans of kitty litter from the trunk, peel off the duct tape, remove the lids, and pour the kitty litter under the wheels of the car.
8. Gently press the gas pedal.

HOW IT WORKS
The kitty litter poured under the tires creates emergency traction for an automobile stuck in snow or on ice.

GAINING TRACTION
- Another way to create traction for a car or truck stuck in snow or on ice: carefully pour a little bleach directly from the jug over the affected tire, wait 1 minute, and then try to move the car. The bleach chemically reacts with the rubber tire, making it stickier, increasing the traction.
- You can also free a car from the snow by placing tree branches or the carpet mats (from inside the car) under the tires.

OFF THE BEATEN TRACK

How to Save on Car Rental Insurance

- The law requires you to have liability insurance when you rent a car. However, if your personal auto insurance policy includes liability insurance, you do not need to take out a policy for liability insurance with the car rental company.
- All the other insurance policies are optional.
- Many credit card companies, including Visa and MasterCard, automatically insure the rental car if you use the credit card to pay for the rental—which means you don't have to buy insurance on the rental car from the rental company. Check with your credit card provider to see if you're covered, and for how much. Credit cards generally offer secondary rental insurance, meaning they only pay for certain damages not covered by your regular automobile insurance.
- Comprehensive and collision insurance, offered by rental car companies, covers the rental car if you are responsible for the damage. Your personal auto insurance policy is unlikely to cover this.
- The collision damage waiver also guarantees that the car rental company will pay for certain damages you cause to the car. This waiver also covers any money that a car rental company stands to lose during the "loss of use" period—when the car is in the shop and cannot be rented out. Most auto insurance policies will not cover this cost.

How to Defrost a Frozen Door Lock with a Drinking Straw

WHAT YOU NEED
- Plastic drinking straw

WHAT TO DO
1. Insert one end of the drinking straw into the key slot.
2. Inhale through your nose and exhale through your mouth into the free end of the straw.
3. Repeat step 2 several times.
4. Remove the straw from the key slot, and try opening the door with the key.

HOW IT WORKS
The hot air you exhale through the straw should easily thaw the lock.

BREAKING THE ICE
Here are a few more ways to defrost a frozen car door lock:
- **Blow Dryer.** If the lock on the car door freezes, before calling a locksmith, use a blow dryer set on hot (with an extension cord), and aim the nozzle at the keyhole to gently thaw the frozen lock.
- **Butane Lighter.** If your car key does not have a plastic top, hold the key with an oven mitt or tongs, and heat the end with a butane lighter. Carefully insert the hot key into the lock to melt the ice inside the tumbler.
- **Cooking Spray.** To prevent car doors from freezing shut in the winter, spray the rubber gaskets with a thin coating of cooking spray. The vegetable oil seals out water without harming the gaskets.
- **Petroleum Jelly.** To prevent a car lock from freezing, dip your key into petroleum jelly, insert it into the lock, and turn the lock back and forth several times. The petroleum jelly, coating the inner parts of the lock, displaces water that would freeze into ice.

How to Repair a Scratch or Ding with Nail Polish

WHAT YOU NEED

- Soapy water
- Soft, clean rag
- Bottle of nail polish, appropriately colored
- Bottle of clear nail polish

WHAT TO DO

1. Using soapy water and a soft, clean rag, wipe any dirt or grime from the ding and surrounding area. (Otherwise, the nail polish will seal in grime.)
2. Make sure the color of the nail polish matches the color of the car.
3. Apply one coat of the nail polish to the ding and let it dry completely.
4. If necessary, apply a second coat of nail polish and let it dry fully.
5. Apply a topcoat of clear nail polish and let it dry.

HOW IT WORKS

The colored nail polish fills the indentation with the proper color, and the topcoat of clear nail polish provides added protection and a fine finish. The nail polish also prevents the metal from rusting and the ding from enlarging.

CAR CARE

"Left untreated, exposed, raw metal on the body of your car can rust in just a matter of weeks," Matt Cutaia, vice president and former body shop manager at Gates Automotive Center in Rochester, New York, told Fox News in 2012. Clear nail polish applied to the ding "may not look the most appealing," said Cutaia, "but you'll have the peace of mind in knowing that rust won't develop quite as quickly."

How to Hot-Wire the Ignition with a Screwdriver

WHAT YOU NEED
- Flat-head screwdriver
- Hammer
- Phillips-head screwdriver
- Car manual
- Rubber gloves
- Wire cutters
- Electrical tape

WHAT TO DO

1. Insert the flat-head screwdriver into the ignition, and hit the screwdriver with a hammer until you can turn it like a key. ***Doing so destroys the ignition cylinder.*** Turn the screwdriver to start the car.

2. If the car fails to start, remove the screwdriver from the ignition.

3. Using the Phillips-head screwdriver, remove the screws from the top and bottom panels holding the steering column.

4. Pry the panels apart (using the flat-head screwdriver, if necessary) to expose the ignition cylinder.

5. Identify the battery and starter wires, located beneath the steering column. The two red wires usually control the power to the car's electrical systems. The one or two brown wires typically connect to the starter. Consult the car manual to verify the color coding of your car's wiring.

6. Wearing rubber gloves, use the wire cutters to carefully cut the power wires from the cylinder.

7. Strip the ends of the power wires, twist them together, and wrap them with electrical tape. If the car has only one starter wire, do not wrap the power wires with electrical tape just yet.

8. Still wearing rubber gloves, use the wire cutters to carefully cut the starter wires from the cylinder.

9. Strip the ends of the starter wires, being careful ***not to let them touch*** and give you an electrical shock. If the car has only one starter wire, strip the end of it.

10. Touch the ends of the starter wires together until the car starts and then pull the wires apart. If the car has only one starter wire, touch it to the connected power wires to start the car.

11. Wrap the two exposed starter wires (or single wire) with electrical tape to prevent them from touching each other while driving.

12. If the steering wheel remains locked in place, insert the flat-head screwdriver between the top of the steering column and the steering wheel to pry open the lock bolt.

13. To turn the engine off, remove the electrical tape holding the power wires together and separate the wires. Wrap the two exposed ends with electrical tape to prevent them from accidentally making contact.

HOW IT WORKS

Twisting the power wires together completes the circuit for the car's electrical system, and holding the starter wires together momentarily circumvents the job of the ignition cylinder—starting the engine.

START ME UP

- Be aware that hot-wiring a car **puts you in danger of electrocution** and is likely to damage your vehicle.
- Hot-wiring anyone's car but your own, without express permission from the owner, is grand theft auto and is usually charged as a felony.
- Newer cars are nearly impossible to hot-wire without professional know-how due to their complex key systems and wheel locks.

How to Break into a Locked Car with a Clothes Hanger

WHAT YOU NEED
- Wire clothes hanger

WHAT TO DO
1. If you get locked out of your own car, unwind and straighten the wire hanger and make a V-shaped hook at the end, roughly 2 inches in length.
2. Slide the hook into the left side of the passenger door between the rubber molding at the bottom of the window and the glass itself.
3. Once you slide the hook into the frame of the car door, rotate the hanger 90 degrees so the open end of the hook faces toward the inside of the car.
4. Gently move the hook up and down and side to side, using the hanger to feel for the arm mechanism inside the frame of the car door that controls the lock.
5. When you locate the arm mechanism, lightly tug upward on the hanger.

HOW IT WORKS
The V-shaped hook on the end of the hanger catches the arm mechanism, and when pulled upward, raises the lock.

DON'T LEAVE ME HANGING

Other clever uses for a wire clothes hanger:

- **Fish for Dropped Objects.** Bend a hook on the end of a straightened hanger, and use it to fish a key chain dropped into a sewer grating, a toy kicked under the furniture, or a sock that fell behind the washing machine.
- **Fix a Drawstring.** Make a loop in the end of a straightened hanger, knot one end of a drawstring to the loop, and use the wire to feed the string and loop through the waistband of a swimsuit or jogging suit.
- **Roast Marshmallows or Hot Dogs.** Skewer some marshmallows or hot dogs on the end of a straightened wire hanger and roast them over a campfire or in a fireplace.
- **Snake Wire.** Make a small loop at one end of a straightened hanger, attach the end of the wire to the loop, drill a series of small holes in the wall, and use the outstretched hanger to snake the wire behind the drywall.
- **Unclog a Drain or Vacuum Cleaner Hose.** Use a straightened wire hanger to dislodge hair and other clogs from a drain or vacuum cleaner hose.

How to Find Your Car in a Parking Lot with a Water Bottle

WHAT YOU NEED

- Wireless key fob (the remote control for your car keys)
- Water bottle filled with water

WHAT TO DO

1. If you cannot remember where you parked your car in a parking lot, hold up your wireless key fob and press the button to activate the car horn.
2. If the horn does not sound, hold the wireless key fob against the side of your head, and press the button to activate the car horn.
3. If the horn still does not sound, hold up a bottle of water, hold the wireless key fob against the side of the water bottle, and press the button to activate the horn in your car.

HOW IT WORKS

A wireless key fob sends out electromagnetic waves at roughly 315 megahertz in North America (with a wavelength of approximately 3 feet) and 434 megahertz in Europe to remotely control the locks, lights, horns, and trunk of an automobile. A wireless key fob has a range of electromagnetic waves extending approximately 188 feet. Holding the fob against your head or a bottle of water when pressing it can extend the range of electromagnetic waves to approximately 440 feet. When the electromagnetic waves pass through the water (in the bottle or our brains), the electric field pulls the positively charged hydrogen ions in one direction and the negatively charged oxygen ions in the opposite direction. The oscillating electric field causes the electrons to radiate energy at the same frequency as the electromagnetic waves from the key, combining to increase the range of the key fob.

OFF THE BEATEN TRACK

How to Get a Great Price on a Rental Car

- **Shop Around Online.** Use websites like Hotwire, Kayak, or Priceline to compare quotes from different car rental companies, whose prices can vary widely.
- **Join a Club.** Members of AAA, AARP, and warehouse club stores (like Costco and Sam's Club) get special rates on rental cars.
- **Avoid Renting at the Airport.** Renting from an airport location generally includes additional fees and taxes that significantly jack up the price. Taking public transportation to an offsite rental car location can save more than 50 percent off the price.
- **Do Not Book at the Counter.** You'll save money and get the size car you want by making a reservation.
- **Reserve a Smaller Car.** Book an economy-size car in advance. If the model you book is unavailable when you show up, the company will upgrade you to a more expensive car for free.
- **Rent by the Week or Longer.** The longer the rental period, the less expensive the daily cost.
- **Aim for the Weekend.** The least expensive rates tend to be the weekend rates.
- **Skip the Optional Extras.** Renting a navigation system or a baby seat from the car rental company adds up quickly. Instead, use an old-fashioned map, Google Maps, MapQuest, or your smart phone. Buying a baby seat can be more economical than renting one.
- **Buy Your Own Gas.** Car rental companies offer you the option of bringing the car back with the gas tank full or buying a full tank of gas in advance at a discounted rate. If you bring the car back with the gas tank half full, you'll still pay for an entire tank of gas. If you do opt to buy your own fuel, save your receipt from the gas station in case the rental company requires proof that you filled up the tank within several miles of the return location.
- **Return the Car on Time.** If you return the car more than an hour late, you'll usually be charged for an extra day.
- **Return the Car at the Agreed-Upon Location.** Returning the car at a different location can result in a large drop-off fee.

How to Grease a Car Axle with Vegetable Oil

WHAT YOU NEED

- Screwdriver or wrench (depending on the differential drain plug)
- Drain pan or plastic storage container
- Funnel
- 2 quarts of vegetable oil

WHAT TO DO

1. In an emergency situation, if you need to replace the differential fluid, use a screwdriver or wrench to remove the differential fill plug, located roughly halfway up the differential in the middle of the rear axle.
2. Place a drain pan or plastic storage container under the differential.
3. Use a screwdriver or wrench to remove the differential drain plug, located on the bottom of the differential.
4. Allow the oil to drain.
5. Replace the drain plug and tighten it securely.
6. Using a funnel, pour 2 quarts of vegetable oil in the fill hole, or until the oil nears the top of the hole.
7. Replace the fill plug and tighten it snugly.

HOW IT WORKS

Vegetable oil doubles as an effective substitute for differential fluid. As soon as you can, replace the vegetable oil with differential fluid that contains additives to help keep the seals, gears, and bearings operating properly.

SPINNING YOUR WHEELS

- The differential, a gearbox located between the drive wheels of the vehicle, works with the transmission to deliver power from the engine to the axle that turns your wheels.
- The differential gears are lubricated with an oil that carries heat away from them, preserving the life and performance of the gears.

- If high operating temperatures cause the differential fluid to deteriorate or if leaks develop, the gears start grinding together, leading to expensive damage.
- In the 1998 movie *Saving Private Ryan*, Captain Miller (Tom Hanks) proposes that his men disable German tanks by making a sticky bomb by filling a standard-issue GI sock with explosive powder, rigging up a fuse, and coating the whole thing with axle grease, creating a bomb that sticks to the tracks of an enemy tank.

EVERY TRICK IN THE BOOK
How to Improvise a Funnel

- **Aluminum Foil.** If you need a funnel in a pinch, double over a piece of aluminum foil and roll it into the shape of a cone.
- **Paper Cup.** Punch a hole in the bottom of a paper cup near the edge to devise an impromptu funnel.
- **Soda Bottle.** To devise a funnel, cut the bottom off a clean, empty plastic soda bottle, turn the upper half upside down, and remove the cap.
- **Ziplock Bag.** Using a pair of scissors, snip off one of the bottom corners from a ziplock freezer bag.

HOW TO MAINTAIN YOUR CAR

- **Change the Oil Regularly.** As the oil ages, the viscosity increases. The engine works harder to circulate the thicker oil, significantly reducing the vehicle's fuel economy. Adhering to scheduled oil changes, keeping the oil at the proper level, and using lower-weight oil helps your engine run smoothly and burn less fuel.
- **Rotate the Tires.** Friction causes the front tires to wear quicker than the rear tires. Rotating the tires equalizes tread wear and prolongs the life of the tires. Most manufacturers recommend rotating the tires approximately every 5,000 to 10,000 miles. See your owner's manual to determine precisely how often and in what pattern to rotate your tires. You can rotate the tires yourself with a torque wrench and a small hydraulic jack (or ideally, a floor jack), or you can bring the car to a mechanic. To make sure the mechanic rotates your tires, use an indelible white marker to draw an inconspicuous white mark on your rear tires. Before you pay the bill, make sure the white mark is on your front tires.

- **Keep the Tires Balanced.** An out-of-balance tire can shorten the life of your tires, bearings, shock absorbers, and other suspension components. If you feel strange vibrations when driving, have your tires checked to make sure they are properly balanced.
- **Do Not Ignore Weird Noises.** Strange noises could indicate the start of a serious problem, which, if ignored, could become costly to fix. Bring the car to a mechanic to assess the problem immediately, and be sure to describe the sound—clumping, knocking, thumping, pinging, screeching, scraping, squealing, rumbling, thudding, ticking, jolting, or whining—and the circumstances that create it as accurately as possible.
- **Do Preventative Maintenance Yourself.** To save money and avoid costly repairs, top off the oil and antifreeze, change worn windshield wiper blades, and replace the air filter yourself, and check the belts and hoses for wear.
- **Check the Tire Pressure Monthly.** Keeping your tires inflated to the proper pressure can improve your gas mileage by up to 3.3 percent, according to the US Department of Energy. Underinflated tires put more stress on the engine and can lower gas mileage by 0.3 percent for every 1 psi (pound per square inch) drop in pressure of all four tires. Properly inflated tires are safer and last longer. Tires lose pressure daily, typically 1 to 2 pounds of air per month. Keep a tire gauge in your glove compartment and check the tire pressure once a month.

How to Prevent Insects from Sticking to the Hood with Cooking Spray

WHAT YOU NEED

- Aerosol cooking spray
- Garden hose (ideally with a high-pressure nozzle)
- Dishwashing liquid
- Bucket
- Water
- Soft sponge

WHAT TO DO
1. Before you set out on your journey, spray the hood and grill of the vehicle with a light coat of cooking spray.
2. After the car trip, simply hose off the hood and grill to wash off any insects.
3. To remove the cooking spray from the hood and grill, simply add a few drops of dishwashing liquid to a bucket filled with water, saturate a sponge in the mixture, and wash the hood and grill.
4. Rinse the car with water from a hose.

HOW IT WORKS
The cooking oil prevents dead insects from permanently adhering to the finish and makes washing them off much simpler. The soapy water made with dishwashing liquid dissolves the vegetable oil.

BUG OFF
- To prevent dead insects from adhering to your windshield, treat the outside of the glass with Rain-X.
- To avoid getting insect carcasses stuck all over your windshield, hood, and grill, drive in the early morning or at night. Winged insects—particularly lovebugs—are most active after mid-morning in bright sunlight when temperatures rise to around 80° Fahrenheit and at dusk.
- Resist the temptation to wash the insects from the windshield with the windshield wipers or the windscreen washer. The attempt will sully the windshield with smears and streaks.
- Wash dead insects from the car exterior as soon as possible. Otherwise, the remains can permanently damage the paint.

OFF THE BEATEN TRACK
How to Save Money on Fuel

- **Drive the Speed Limit.** When you drive above 38 miles per hour in most cars, you decrease your mileage. For every 5 miles per hour you drive above 55 miles per hour, you lose up to 10 percent of your fuel economy. The slower you go, the less gas you burn. Each 5 MPH you drive over 60 MPH is like paying an additional 28 cents per gallon for gas, according to the US Department of Energy.
- **Minimize the Number of Trips You Make.** Instead of making several short round-trip journeys (to the bank, to the mall, to the post office), combine all your errands into one big trip, drive to your farthest destination first (to get the engine running efficiently), and work your way back home. Use a map to plan an efficient itinerary, or download the free smart phone app Maps + Compass.
- **Avoid Getting Stuck in Traffic.** The more time you spend stuck in bumper-to-bumper traffic, the more fuel you waste. To monitor traffic, download a traffic app like Aha, Waze, TrafficTweet, or Google Maps Navigation, which give real-time traffic conditions on major roads and highways.
- **Take a Less Grueling Route.** Instead of taking the long and winding scenic route over hill and dale, choose a route with smooth, level roads and less traffic lights or stop signs. A longer route with less arduous road conditions necessitates less gas.
- **Lay Off the Pedals.** By accelerating slowly and evenly and going easy on the brakes (coasting whenever possible), you can cut your fuel consumption by 35 percent, according to the Environmental Protection Agency and a road test conducted by Edmunds.com. When approaching a red light or a stop sign, lift your foot off the gas pedal as soon as possible, allowing the car to coast. When you encounter traffic congestion, instead of accelerating from 0 to 20 and then braking back to 0, maintain a steady speed and let the car in front of you move ahead; you'll catch up when the traffic inevitably slows back down.
- **Lighten Your Load.** The more your car weighs, the harder the engine works, consuming more gasoline. Remove the ice chests, beach chairs, and bowling balls from your trunk and backseat. An extra 100 pounds reduces a typical car's fuel economy by 1 to 2 percent. If you're driving a van without any passengers aboard, store the two backseats in your garage to remove excess weight.

Remove any add-ons, like flags, bicycle carriers, and luggage racks, which undermine the vehicle's aerodynamics, increasing your gasoline consumption.

- **Never Leave the Car Running.** Letting your car idle for 15 minutes while you wait in front of the school for your kids or while you run into the store to buy something can burn a quarter of a gallon of gasoline, especially if the air-conditioner is running. Turn off the engine, and if you're waiting in the car, simply roll down the windows.

- **Drive a Stick Shift.** Cars and trucks with stick shifts typically get two to five more miles to the gallon than those same vehicles with automatic transmissions, according to *Consumer Reports*. A stick-shift car generally costs $800 to $1,200 less and demands fewer and less expensive brake and transmission repairs. To give your stick-shift vehicle more mileage, shift slowly and stay in low gears.

- **Use Cruise Control.** When driving on the highway, you'll get better mileage using cruise control than your right foot. In a test conducted by Edmunds.com, a Land Rover LR3 got almost 14 percent better mileage and a Ford Mustang got 4.5 percent better mileage using cruise control set at 70 miles per hour rather than cruising at driver-controlled speeds between 65 and 75 miles per hour. Using cruise control prevents fluctuations in speed and "speed creep"—the tendency of a driver to gradually accelerate over time.

- **Play the Water Game.** Place a cup filled with water in the cup holder and drive without spilling it. You'll avoid making abrupt starts and stops, and you'll drive at lower speeds, increasing your city mileage by 5 percent, according to the US Department of Energy.

- **Roll Down the Windows—Unless You're Driving on the Highway.** Running the air-conditioning increases fuel consumption by roughly 10 percent, and while driving with the windows open increases drag and raises fuel consumption, it's the less costly of the two evils—when you're driving in the city. When you're driving on the highway, the opposite is true. Running the air conditioner at highway speeds has less effect on fuel economy than rolling down the windows, according to Edmunds.com.

- **Park in the Sun.** Parking your vehicle in the sun on a cold day keeps your car warmer, enabling the engine to warm up rapidly, running more efficiently and using less gas.

How to Improvise an Ice Scraper with a Spatula

WHAT YOU NEED
- Plastic spatula
- Broom

WHAT TO DO

1. ***Remove any snow or ice obstructing the vehicle's tailpipe.*** Otherwise, running the engine can fill the inside of the vehicle with poisonous carbon monoxide gas.
2. Start the vehicle and turn on the defroster to slowly warm the glass windshield.
3. Let the car warm up for at least 5 minutes.
4. When the ice frozen to the windshield starts melting, use the plastic spatula to gently scrape off the ice.
5. Use the broom to sweep the ice scrapings from the windshield and hood.

HOW IT WORKS
The defroster helps melt the ice, loosening it from the glass, and the spatula doubles as an effective ice scraper.

WALKING ON THIN ICE
If your windshield gets covered with ice, mix 10 ounces of isopropyl alcohol and 5 ounces of cool water in a 16-ounce trigger-spray bottle. Spray this homemade deicing solution on the iced windows, and the ice will peel right off.

EVERY TRICK IN THE BOOK

Breaking the Ice

If you don't have an ice scraper, here are several items you can use to do the job.

- **Credit Card.** Use an expired credit card or any sturdy laminated card to scrape the ice and snow away. Avoid using a valid credit card that might get damaged by the scraping.
- **Dustpan.** A plastic dustpan does the scraping job without scratching the windshield.
- **Plastic Lid.** The edge of a lid from a coffee can works just like a scraper.
- **Paint Scraper.** Grab a plastic paint scraper from your workshop to scrape the ice off your windshield.

How to Escape from the Trunk of a Car with a Car Jack

WHAT YOU NEED

- Car jack

WHAT TO DO

1. If the trunk is not equipped with a working release switch, search the walls of the trunk or under the false bottom of the trunk for the jack.
2. Position the jack on the floor of the trunk under the center section of the lid near the latch.
3. If using a scissor jack, insert the rod or wrench over the knob, and then crank. If using a hydraulic jack, place the handle into the appropriate slot and pump up and down with slow, even strokes.
4. Crank or pump the jack until the trunk lid pops open.

HOW IT WORKS

The force of the jack forces the trunk lid to pop open.

OTHER WAYS OUT OF THE TRUNK

- **Trunk Release Switch.** American cars manufactured after 2002 contain a trunk release switch (usually with a glow-in-the-dark handle) inside the trunk. Locate the button, cord, handle, or toggle switch and engage it to pop open the trunk.
- **Backseat.** If the car you're trapped inside has a backseat that folds down to gain access to the trunk, kick the back of the seat to push it open.

- **Trunk Release Cable.** If the car is equipped with a trunk release lever by the driver's seat, the cable from that switch runs along the driver's side of the car and the side of the trunk, and sometimes on the floor of the trunk. Feel for the cable, and pull up the false bottom of the trunk if necessary. If you locate the cable, pull it toward the front of the car to release the trunk.
- **Brake Lights.** If necessary, pull or pry off the panel covering access to the brake lights. Pull out the wires to the brake lights, and push or kick the lights out of the vehicle. Stick your hand through the hole to signal other motorists. If you fail to push out the lights, disconnecting the wires increases the chances that the police will pull over the driver for a faulty taillight.

Taxis: The Meter Is Running

Here are some tips on how to travel safely in a taxi.

- **Do Your Homework.** Ask a hotel clerk, restaurant manager, or store clerk for the typical price range of a taxi ride to your destination, and the proper tip.
- **Set the Price Up Front.** When you get into the taxi, either make sure the driver is using the meter or agree upon the flat fare before you start the journey. Most dispatchers can give you a ballpark price when you book a taxi.
- **Know How to Get There.** Familiarize yourself with the general direction, the best route, and the travel time to your destination. If the taxi driver heads the wrong way, give the driver proper directions, insist that he stop the meter until he gets on the right road, or—if you're in a safe neighborhood—get out of the cab. If appropriate, toss some money into the front seat to prevent any hard feelings.
- **Play It Smart.** If the taxi driver asks you if you've been to the city before, say yes. Otherwise, a dishonest driver may take a longer route to jack up the metered fare.
- **Telephone for a Taxi Instead of Hailing One.** Calling a dispatcher helps minimize the chances of getting an unscrupulous independent taxi driver.

- **Record the Numbers.** Before getting into a taxi, memorize the company's name and the taxi number (usually painted on the outside of the cab).
- **Never Get into a Taxi if a Stranger Is in the Passenger Seat.** For starters, you shouldn't be paying for a stranger's ride, and the driver and the stranger may be in cahoots to rob passengers.
- **Do Not Sit in the Front Passenger Seat.** Sitting in the backseat keeps you at a safe distance from the driver.
- **Make Sure the Driver's Taxi License Is Prominently Displayed.** Otherwise, do not get into the taxi.
- **Locate the Inside Door Handle and Make Sure It Works.** Know how to get out of the vehicle.
- **Do Not Take a Taxi Alone if You're Drunk.** Yes, you should take a taxi rather than drive, but take a taxi with a friend. Otherwise, you will be vulnerable to attack from the driver or any other assailant.
- **Keep Expensive Items Hidden on Your Person or on the Floor Between Your Feet.** Flashing a smart phone, camera, jewelry, purse, daypack, or a wallet makes you a target for potential thieves.
- **Keep the Windows Closed.** This prevents a thief from reaching into an open window or opening a locked door at a traffic light or stop sign.
- **Familiarize Yourself with the Local Currency.** If you're in a foreign country, pay with the correct denomination bills and make sure the driver gives you change in the proper currency.

How to Fog-Proof Your Windshield with Shaving Cream and a Maxi Pad

WHAT YOU NEED
- Can of shaving cream
- Maxi pad

WHAT TO DO
1. Fill your palm with a handful of shaving cream.
2. Rub a thin coating of the shaving cream on the inside of the windshield.
3. Using the maxi pad, wipe the shaving cream off the glass.

HOW IT WORKS
The thin coating of emollients the shaving cream leaves on the inside of the windshield prevent the glass from fogging.

EVERY TRICK IN THE BOOK
Close Shave

You can also use shaving cream in the following ways:

- **Baseball Glove Softener.** To break in a new baseball glove, rub the center of the glove with shaving cream, place a baseball in the glove, fold the mitt around it, and secure it with rubber bands. Tuck the glove under a mattress overnight.
- **Carpet Spot Remover.** Squirt a dab of shaving cream on the stain, scrub, and wash with water.
- **Hand Cleaner.** Rubbing shaving cream between your hands will dissolve grease, grime, and latex paint without water. Keep a can of it at the workbench.
- **Ski Goggle Defogger.** Spray with shaving cream, then wipe clean.
- **Squeaky Hinge Lubricant.** Spray the joint with shaving cream.
- **Upholstery Cleaner.** Apply shaving cream sparingly to the stain and rub gently with a damp cloth.

How to Recharge a Dead Car Battery with Red Wine

WHAT YOU NEED

- Safety goggles
- Rubber gloves
- Screwdriver
- Funnel
- Red wine

WHAT TO DO

1. To revive a dead car battery, wear safety goggles and rubber gloves, and carefully pry the cell cover off the battery with a screwdriver (without getting battery acid on yourself).
2. Using a funnel, pour a little red wine into each of the battery cells.
3. Reseal the cell cover.
4. Let the car sit for no more than one hour, and start the engine.
5. Drive directly to a service station to replace the battery.

HOW IT WORKS

If the battery levels get too low, the cells drain, and the vehicle will not start. Red wine is an acidic liquid that allows the electrons to flow freely between the positive and negative terminals of the battery, providing sufficient energy to start the engine.

WINE

- In an episode of *MacGyver* ("Jack of Lies," season 2, episode 6), MacGyver unscrews the caps on a dead car battery, pours wine into the battery, replaces the caps, and starts the engine.
- In 2010, Japanese scientists working with superconductors discovered that hot commercial alcoholic beverages, including red wine, white wine, beer, sake, and whiskey, induced superconductivity in $FeTe_{0.8}S_{0.2}$. The scientists achieved the largest shielding volume fraction using red wine.
- If you need to disconnect your car's negative battery cable to work on the engine, you must prevent the live end of the battery cable connector from touching the car frame or other metal. To do this, cut a slit in a tennis ball and carefully insert the negative battery connector into the rubber ball. Since the rubber tennis ball does not conduct electricity, you can safely place the encapsulated battery connector aside.

OFF THE BEATEN TRACK
How to Lower Your Car Insurance

- **Keep Your Driving Record Clean.** The best way to lower your automobile insurance is to keep a safe driving record. Drivers with a clean record can save up to 45 percent with Allstate, up to 26 percent with Geico, and up to 10 percent with State Farm.
- **Buy a Safe, Reliable Car.** A vehicle renowned for its expensive repairs, popularity with thieves, or questionable safety record tends to be expensive to insure. Before buying a new car, check the vehicle's risk level at the Insurance Institute for Highway Safety's website, www.iihs.org.
- **Insure Your Car, House, and Life Through the Same Company.** To lower the cost of your car insurance, purchasing your car insurance from the same company that provides your homeowner's policy and/or life insurance policy can save 10 to 15 percent.
- **Take Higher Deductibles.** Increasing your deductible (the amount of money you must pay before your insurance policy kicks in) can significantly lower the cost of your collision and comprehensive coverage. Raising your deductible from $200 to $1,000 can lower the cost of insurance by at least 40 percent. Do the math to determine if the reduced premium saves you more than the cost of the deductible.
- **Drop Unnecessary Coverage.** If you own an older car with a low market value, calculate whether any claim you make will exceed the cost of the insurance and your deductible. If it doesn't, consider discontinuing collision and/or comprehensive coverage. You can determine your car's current value at Kelley Blue Book (kbb.com) or Edmunds.com.
- **Participate in a Driver Safety Program.** Many insurance companies give a 5 to 10 percent discount for taking part in the AARP Driver Safety Program (aarpdriversafety.org) or teenSMART, the teen crash reduction program.
- **Pay Your Bill Up Front or with Automatic Payments.** Many insurance companies give discounts for paying your annual premium in full or paying by automatic withdrawal.
- **Avoid Buying Duplicate Medical Coverage.** If you already have extensive health, life, and disability insurance, consider reducing the medical coverage in your car insurance policy to the minimum personal injury protection required by your state. Medical coverage in your auto insurance policy also pays for injuries incurred to passengers in your car, so carefully consider whether to limit that coverage based on how frequently you transport others.

- **Question the Need for Roadside Assistance.** Before you purchase an insurance policy that includes roadside assistance, check to see whether your credit card already provides free roadside assistance. A roadside assistance plan purchased elsewhere (perhaps through AAA) may be less expensive than through your insurance carrier, especially if a tow or jump-start raises your insurance premium or tarnishes your eligibility for coverage.
- **Pay Less for Driving Less.** If you work at home, carpool frequently, or ride public transportation to work, call your insurance company to ask if you quality for a low-mileage discount based on the number of miles you drive annually.
- **Upgrade the Safety Equipment.** Most insurance companies give discounts if your car is equipped with passive restraints (air bags and motorized seatbelts), antilock brakes, or an antitheft device.
- **Ask for Discounts for Teenage Drivers.** Insuring teenagers on the parents' policy costs less than buying a separate policy, and teenagers who pass an approved drivers education course can qualify for discount rates. A single full-time student under 25 with a minimum 3.0 GPA can save up to 15 percent with Geico, up to 20 percent with Allstate, and up to 35 percent with State Farm. A college student who attends school more than 100 miles from home and does not bring a car may quality for an additional discount.
- **Shop Around.** Call several insurance companies to compare rates and get the lowest premiums.

How to Heat Up a Frozen TV Dinner on a Car Manifold

WHAT YOU NEED

- Aluminum foil
- TV dinner
- Pliers (or wire cutters)
- Wire coat hanger
- Tongs, an oven mitt, or potholders

WHAT TO DO

1. Drive for a few minutes to warm up your engine, then pull over, park, and turn off the engine.
2. Open the hood and locate hot metal spots on the engine. Generally, the best spot on the engine for cooking food is on or near the exhaust manifold on top of the injector housing.
3. Crumple up a sheet of aluminum foil into a ball roughly 6 inches in diameter. Place the ball on the spot you wish to use as a grill and close the hood. Reopen the hood and compare the crumpled ball to your TV dinner tray to make sure you'll have sufficient height to cook your TV dinner tray.
4. Wrap the aluminum tray of the TV dinner in a sheet of aluminum foil.
5. Place the wrapped TV dinner on the engine, away from any moving parts.
6. Using a pair of pliers, trim a piece of wire hanger so you can use wire to secure the TV dinner in place without placing any strain on the hoses.
7. Place a crumpled-up ball of aluminum foil on top of the package to hold it in place when you close the hood.
8. Turn the ignition and drive the car or truck for roughly 30 minutes.
9. Park the car and turn off the engine.
10. Use tongs, an oven mitt, or potholders to carefully remove the food from the hot engine.
11. Carefully unwrap the aluminum foil and serve.

HOW IT WORKS

The heat produced by the car engine manifold while driving defrosts and heats the TV dinner. The engine can also heat any foil-wrapped foods.

NOW YOU'RE COOKING

- Cooking times for cooking on your car manifold are generally longer than in a conventional oven.
- Locomotive engineers used to heat their food on the steam engine manifolds, and truck drivers frequently cook using their diesel engine manifold.
- In 2013, local blues folk musician Charlie Parr told *Minneapolis City Pages* that he uses a can of lentil beans and a bag of frozen veggies to cook on his manifold. "I use some curry powder, garlic, cayenne pepper, and mix it all up. Wrap it in foil, two layers but no more than four, like it's a bowl with all the opening parts up. Before you close it add a bit of water, maybe a ¼ cup—not much. Jam it onto the exhaust manifold, making sure it's making good contact and not in the way of any moving parts or in danger of falling off. Use a little wire if necessary. Then start the motor and double check that nothing's being impeded by your dinner. Drive away. If it's hot outside, go about 20–25 miles and check it and give it a stir. Another 25–50 miles would do it for me."
- The classic cookbook *Manifold Destiny: The One! The Only! Guide to Cooking on Your Car Engine!* by Chris Maynard and Bill Scheller, explains how to prepare tasty dishes on your vehicle's engine. The book includes recipes for Hyundai Halibut, Prius Pork, Thruway Chicken Thighs, and Ford F-150 Hot Texas Wieners.

How to Park a Car in a Garage with a Tennis Ball

WHAT YOU NEED
- Chalk
- Ladder
- Safety goggles
- Drill with ⅛-inch bit
- 2 eye screws
- String
- Tennis ball
- Scissors

WHAT TO DO
1. Park the car in the garage in the proper location.
2. Look at the windshield and identify the location of the rearview mirror mount.
3. On the garage floor in front of the car, make a chalk mark perpendicular to the rearview mirror mount.
4. On the garage floor on the side of the car, make a chalk mark perpendicular to the rearview mirror mount.
5. Remove the car from the garage.
6. Using the two chalk marks on the floor as a guide, make a chalk X on the floor directly under the spot where the rearview mirror mount was.
7. Using a ladder and wearing safety goggles, climb up to the ceiling and drill a small starter hole into the ceiling or rafter directly above the chalk X on the floor.
8. Carefully twist one eye screw into the hole.
9. Thread one end of the string through the eye screw, allowing the opposite end of the string to touch the floor, and tie several knots to secure the string to the eye screw.
10. Put the ladder away, and park the car inside the garage in its proper location, allowing the string to fall loosely on the windshield.
11. Wearing safety goggles, carefully drill a small hole in the tennis ball.
12. Insert an eye screw into the hole and twist it into place.
13. Standing on a step stool if necessary, thread the free end of the string through the eye screw on the tennis ball, and adjust the height of the ball so it touches the windshield when hanging straight.

14. Tie several knots to secure the string to the eye screw on the ball.

15. Using a pair of scissors, carefully trim the excess string.

HOW IT WORKS

To park the car in your garage without hitting the far garage wall accidentally, drive forward until the tennis ball touches the windshield.

7

RECREATIONAL VEHICLES AND CAMPERS

You're driving your RV across Kansas, with another 220 miles before the next town. The windshield's covered with road grime, the microwave oven reeks of burnt popcorn, one of your companions spilled a glass of wine on the carpet, and your neck hurts from all that driving. All you've got in the RV is a bottle of Coca-Cola, some lemons, a canister of salt, and a box of rice. What do you do?

How to Avoid Losing Keys with a Fishing Bobber

WHAT YOU NEED

- Snap-on fishing bobber, 1¾-inch diameter
- Needle-nose pliers
- 25-pound-test fishing line, 6 inches long
- Paint, indelible markers, rub-on transfers, or rhinestones

WHAT TO DO

1. Push the red trigger mechanism on the top of the white half of the bobber, and using the needle-nose pliers, straighten the thin wire hook at the bottom of the red half of the bobber.

2. Pull out the trigger mechanism and the accompanying wire and spring.

3. Feed the end of the fishing line through the small hole in the bottom of the red half of the bobber and out the hole in the white half of the bobber.

4. Tie the two ends of the fishing line to each other, making a tight knot.

5. Using the needle-nose pliers, snip off the excess fishing line beyond the knot.

6. Attach your key ring to the loop of fishing line on the outside of the bobber.

7. If desired, personalize the bobber with paint, indelible markers, rub-on transfers, or rhinestones.

HOW IT WORKS

The buoyant fishing bobber keeps several keys from sinking to the bottom of the lake should they be accidentally dropped overboard.

EVERY TRICK IN THE BOOK

Fishing for Compliments

Fishing bobbers can be used for several fun craft projects:

- **Christmas Tree Ornaments.** Make a Santa Claus head or a snowman from classic red-and-white fishing bobbers. To create a Santa ornament, glue some cotton to the bottom white half of a large bobber to make a beard, a small cotton ball on top of the red half to make a hat, and a pair of googly eyes. For a snowman, connect a small, medium, and large bobber by their hooks and then use an indelible marker to give your snowman eyes and shirt buttons. Feed thin ribbon through the top hook to hang the ornaments.
- **Christmas Wreaths.** Wrap white Christmas lights around a wire wreath form, and cover the form by attaching various-sized red-and-white fishing bobbers.
- **Earrings.** Attach earring clasps to the top of two fishing bobbers and you've got a pair of fashionable earrings.
- **Light Pull.** Use the hook atop the bobber to attach it to the existing light chain.
- **Refrigerator Magnets.** Use a hot glue gun to attach a magnet to a fishing bobber.

How to Protect a Trailer Hitch with a Tennis Ball

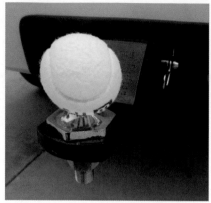

WHAT YOU NEED

- Knife or pair of scissors
- Tennis ball

WHAT TO DO

1. Using a knife or pair of scissors, cut a large X in the tennis ball.
2. When you are not using the vehicle for towing a trailer, hold the X over the trailer hitch ball.
3. Push hard until the tennis ball pops onto the trailer hitch ball.

HOW IT WORKS

The tennis ball covers the metal trailer hitch ball, preventing it from getting scratched or damaged. The tennis ball cover also prevents you from rubbing up against the greased hitch.

ON THE BALL

- To avoid bumping your head on the latch under the hood, carefully cut a slot in a tennis ball and place it over the latch. Should you bump your head, the tennis ball will soften the blow.
- If you need to disconnect your car's negative battery cable to work on the engine, it's important to prevent the live end of the battery cable connector from touching the car frame or other metal surface. Cut a slit in a tennis ball and carefully insert the negative battery connector into the rubber ball. Since the rubber tennis ball does not conduct electricity, you can safely place the encapsulated battery connector aside.
- To keep your car door open without wasting the battery, wedge a tennis ball into the doorjamb to depress the interior light switch.

How to Prevent Mold and Mildew with Kitty Litter

WHAT YOU NEED
- Kitty litter
- 2 plastic storage containers (approximately 10 inches wide by 15 inches long by 6 inches deep) or shallow cardboard box

WHAT TO DO
1. To prevent mold and mildew from accumulating in a locked-up RV, pour unused kitty litter in two plastic storage containers (or a shallow cardboard box), roughly 2 inches deep.
2. Place one plastic container inside the bathtub or shower stall, and place the second container on the floor of the kitchen.
3. Lock up the RV for the season. (If you have cats, make sure the doors to the RV remain closed so the cats don't use the kitty litter in the tubs.)

HOW IT WORKS
The kitty litter absorbs moisture and musty, lingering odors, preventing mold and mildew from growing.

How to Keep Your RV Cool with Space Blankets

WHAT YOU NEED
- Scissors
- Space blankets
- Scotch tape (or packaging or duct tape)

WHAT TO DO
1. Using scissors, carefully cut the space blankets to the size of the inside of the windowpanes and windshield—with the shiny side of the space blanket facing toward the glass.
2. Using Scotch tape, adhere the space blankets to the insides of the windows—again, with the shiny side of the space blankets facing toward the glass.
3. When you remove the sheets of space blanket from the windows, save the sheets for reuse.

HOW IT WORKS
The space blankets reflect up to 80 percent of radiant heat, rather than allowing it to pass through the glass into the camper. The metallic surfaces reflect the heat of the sun out of the vehicle.

SECURITY BLANKET
To heat the RV with a space blanket, cover the inside of the windowpanes with sheets of the space blanket with the shiny side facing inward to reflect your body heat back inside the vehicle.

EVERY TRICK IN THE BOOK

Cool Uses for a Space Blanket

Invented in 1964 after a scientist at the National Research Corporation discovered that the metalized sheets of film used as external insulation on satellites and the lunar module could also keep people warm by reflecting heat back to the body, the space blanket has a wide array of alternative uses.

- **Emergency Shelter.** In an emergency, use a space blanket to create an emergency shelter, such as a tent, tarp, or lean-to. The waterproof material repels rain and snow.
- **First Aid.** A space blanket can be used in an emergency situation for its intended purpose of keeping someone warm or preventing an individual from going into shock. To do so, wrap the blanket around the person, tucking in the sides under the body to retain heat and repel cold. To prevent additional heat loss, place a hat on the person's head.
- **Heat Reflector.** To combat cold temperatures, hang the blanket behind a fire or radiator so the shiny side reflects the heat back to you to help keep you warm.
- **Signal Mirror.** If you need to signal for help, use the reflective, shiny surface of the blanket as a signal mirror.
- **Snow Goggles.** Cut a strip of the space blanket and wrap it around your head as a pair of goggles. The see-through material doubles as sunglasses.
- **Sun Shade.** Hang the space blanket like a tarp with the shiny side facing upward to reflect sunlight and heat.
- **Tent Cooler.** To stay cool in a tent pitched in bright sunlight, cover the tent with the space blanket with the shiny side facing upward. The metallic surface reflects the heat away from the tent.
- **Windbreaker.** To protect yourself from cold winds, wrap a space blanket around your shoulders with the shiny side facing your body.

How to Clean Scuff Marks from Floors with a Tennis Ball

WHAT YOU NEED
- Utility knife or sharp scissors
- Tennis ball
- Broomstick

WHAT TO DO
1. Using the utility knife, carefully cut an X in the side of the tennis ball.
2. Unscrew the broomstick from the bristles.
3. Insert the end of the broomstick into the X in the tennis ball.
4. Use the ball at the end of the broomstick like a giant pencil eraser to erase the scuff marks from tile, vinyl, and laminate floors in your RV.

HOW IT WORKS
The rough texture of the tennis ball erases scuff marks from floors, and the broomstick makes the job easier, so you don't have to get down on your hands and knees with just a tennis ball. The janitorial staffs of large buildings use this handy trick.

ROLLING ON THE FLOOR
Other ways to remove scuff marks:
- **Cooking Spray.** To remove scuff marks from the floor, spray the marks with cooking spray and wipe them clean.
- **Mayonnaise.** Use a dab of mayonnaise to clean black scuff marks from a tile or vinyl floor.
- **Nail Polish Remover.** Gently rub the scuff mark with a cotton ball saturated with nail polish remover, then wipe any residue clean with soapy water.
- **Petroleum Jelly.** Rub a dab of petroleum jelly on scuff marks on vinyl or tile floors and buff them with a soft, clean cloth.
- **Toothpaste and Toothbrush.** Squeeze some toothpaste on a clean, used toothbrush (or sponge) and scrub scuff marks off the floor. The toothpaste is a mild abrasive that quickly cleans scuff marks.
- **Vegetable Oil.** Put a few drops of vegetable oil on a soft, clean cloth or a paper towel and gently rub the scuff mark away.

How to Clean Carpet Stains with Salt

WHAT YOU NEED

- 1 or 2 disposable diapers
- Heavy object
- Bottle of club soda
- Sponge
- Canister of salt
- Broom (or whisk broom)
- Vacuum cleaner

WHAT TO DO

1. Blot up the stain immediately to prevent the liquid from spreading and soaking into the padding. Whatever you do, don't let a carpet stain dry. Once the stain dries, it usually becomes permanent.
2. To blot up the spill from the carpet, place a disposable diaper facedown over the stain and place a heavy object on top of the diaper to hold it in place for 10 to 15 minutes.
3. Pour a small amount of club soda on the stain, rub gently with a sponge, and then continue blotting with a disposable diaper. Repeat if necessary.
4. If you're not satisfied with the results, pour a mountain of salt over the stain to cover it completely, wait 15 minutes for the salt to absorb the stain from the carpet, and then sweep up the salt. Repeat if necessary.
5. Use a vacuum cleaner to remove any remaining salt from the carpet.

HOW IT WORKS

The superabsorbent polymer flakes in the disposable diaper absorb 300 times their weight in liquid, sucking up messy spills quickly. The sodium bicarbonate in the club soda causes the liquid in the stain to bubble to the surface where you want it, rather than sinking down into the padding, where you definitely do not want it. Salt is amazingly absorbent and sucks any remaining liquid from the carpet.

SWEEPING IT UNDER THE CARPET

Other ways to clean carpet stains:

- **Ammonia.** To clean stubborn stains from carpet, mix 2 cups of ammonia in 1 gallon of warm water, dampen a sponge with the solution, rub it into the stain gently, and then blot it up with paper towels.

- **Baby Wipes.** To lift minor stains out of the carpet, gently rub them with a baby wipe.
- **Borax.** Blot up a spill, sprinkle borax to cover the area, let it dry, and vacuum it up. (Before treating, test an inconspicuous spot on the carpeting with a paste made from borax and water to make sure the borax does not remove any color from the carpet.)
- **Cornstarch.** To clean spills from the carpet, sprinkle cornstarch over the spot, wait 30 minutes, and then vacuum it clean.
- **Laundry Detergent.** Mix one tablespoon of liquid laundry detergent with 2 cups of water. Scrub the stain with this color-safe solution. Rinse it with cool water, blot, and let it dry.
- **Shaving Cream.** To remove stains from carpet, spray some shaving cream over the spot, scrub it with a wet scrub brush, and then rinse it with a wet cloth to blot up the extra foam.
- **WD-40.** To clean grease, tar, or oil-based paint from carpet, spray a clean cloth with WD-40 and scrub the spot. To remove the grease stain from the WD-40 from the carpeting, use a few drops of dishwashing liquid and some water, scrub lightly, and then blot it up with a paper towel.
- **White Bread.** If you spill oil or grease on your carpet, rub a slice of white bread over the spot to absorb the oil or grease, then vacuum up the crumbs.
- **Window Cleaner.** To clean food or juice stains from carpet, blot up as much of the stain as possible, spray the affected area with window cleaner, and then wipe it clean with a cloth or paper towel.

How to Protect the Carpeting from Slide-Outs with Plastic Cutting Boards

WHAT YOU NEED
- Safety goggles
- Circular saw
- 2 plastic cutting boards (for each slide-out)
- Duct tape

WHAT TO DO

1. To prevent the slide-outs in your RV from rubbing against the carpet and abrading it, wear safety goggles and use a circular saw to carefully cut a plastic cutting board in half lengthwise.
2. Using duct tape, tape the two strips of plastic end to end.
3. Repeat steps 1 and 2 with the second cutting board.
4. Place the first strip under the foot of one wall of the slide-out.
5. Place the second strip under the opposite foot of the slide-out wall.

HOW IT WORKS

When you operate the slide-outs on your RV, rolling them in or out, the carpets generally take a beating. Because most slide-outs do not sit perfectly square, one side presses particularly harder than the other on the carpeting. Plastic cutting boards are thin enough to fit under the foot of the walls, yet thick enough to protect the carpets.

A CUT ABOVE

- A plastic cutting board is better than a wooden cutting board when it comes to preparing meat and seafood. Bacteria from these foods can get trapped in the grain of the porous wood. Plastic is nonporous, and a simple washing with soap and water cleans the surface.
- Placing a damp towel or kitchen cloth under your cutting board keeps the board from slipping, creating a sturdy surface and preventing accidents.

How to Pad Awning Struts with Pool Noodles

WHAT YOU NEED
- Utility knife
- 1 pool noodle for each awning strut

WHAT TO DO

1. Using a utility knife, carefully cut a slit lengthwise in each foam pool noodle.
2. Slip each prepared pool noodle over each awning strut.

HOW IT WORKS

The polyethylene foam creates padding to protect you from injury should you accidentally bump into an awning strut. The foam noodle also prevents the trailer door from slamming against the awning strut.

NOODLE OVER IT

- Pool noodles work well for wedging padding between objects in drawers and cupboards aboard an RV to prevent them from sliding around.
- Using a utility knife, cut a 1-foot length from a pool noodle, carefully cut a slit lengthwise, and slip it around the leg of a dining room table in your RV. The foam noodle protects you from accidently banging your bare feet into the table leg.

How to Clean Road Grime from the Windshield with Coca-Cola

WHAT YOU NEED
- Thumbtack
- Bottle of Coca-Cola
- Squeegee (if available)
- Water

WHAT TO DO
1. Use a thumbtack to punch a hole in the center of the top of a bottle of Coca-Cola.
2. Place your thumb over the hole in the top of the Coca-Cola bottle, and shake the bottle vigorously.
3. Aiming the bottle at the windshield, release your thumb, allowing the Real Thing to spray all over the grease and grime on the windshield, being careful not to let the Coca-Cola come in contact with the paint.
4. Use a squeegee to scrub the grime away.
5. Rinse the windshield clean with water. Be sure to rinse any Coca-Cola from the paint. The acids in the soft drink will etch into it.

HOW IT WORKS
The carbonation, phosphoric acid, citric acid, and ascorbic acid in the Coca-Cola dissolve the greasy film from the windshield.

THE PAUSE THAT REFRESHES
- Since 1920, the Coca-Cola sign has been a continuously changing landmark in New York City's Times Square. The sign has featured neon lighting since 1923. The Coca-Cola bottle unveiled on the billboard in 1991 and displayed for 13 years was the world's largest Coca-Cola

bottle. The Coca-Cola billboard unveiled in 2004 is one of the largest digital canvases in the world, measuring more than six stories high and illuminating more than 2.6 million light-emitting diodes.

- The 1961 madcap comedy *One, Two, Three* stars James Cagney as a Coca-Cola bottler in West Berlin during the Cold War who tries to prevent his American boss's daughter from marrying an East Berlin communist.

- In the 1964 Stanley Kubrick movie *Dr. Strangelove or: How I Learned to Stop Worrying and Love the Bomb*, Peter Sellers instructs his sidekick to shoot the lock off a Coca-Cola vending machine to get the change to make a phone call to the president to prevent a nuclear war. The sidekick warns him, "You're gonna have to answer to the Coca-Cola Company."

- The 1971 Coca-Cola television commercial, featuring the song "I'd Like to Buy the World a Coke" was filmed on a hilltop in Rome, Italy, and featured 500 young people from around the world, hired from embassies and schools in Rome. The close-up shots, however, were filmed at a racetrack in Rome. For the commercial, the British group the New Seekers sang the song—written by Bill Backer, Billy Davis, Roger Cook, and Roger Greenaway—and recorded a retitled version of the song for national release as "I'd Like to Teach the World to Sing (in Perfect Harmony)," which become a top-ten hit. The Coca-Cola Company donated the first $80,000 of royalties earned from the song to UNICEF.

- The 1980 South African comedy *The Gods Must Be Crazy* follows the adventures of a remote bushman who mistakes an empty Coke bottle tossed from an airplane as a gift from the gods.

- The 1985 Australian movie *The Coca-Cola Kid* stars Eric Roberts as an American Coca-Cola executive from Georgia sent to the Australian outback to market the soft drink.

- In July 1985, Coca-Cola became the first soft drink consumed in space aboard a space shuttle mission.

How to Make Waste-Tank Cleaner with Borax and Water Softener

WHAT YOU NEED

- 1 cup of 20 Mule Team Borax
- ½ cup of Calgon water softener
- Bucket

WHAT TO DO

1. Rather than buying toxic and expensive chemicals to clean your RV waste tank, mix 1 cup of 20 Mule Team Borax and ½ cup of Calgon water softener in a bucket.
2. After emptying the waste tank, pour the solution into the tank.

HOW IT WORKS

The borax controls odors and simultaneously cleans the tank. The water softener contains a powerful surfactant that boosts the solvency of water, preventing sewage from sticking to the interior walls of the waste tank.

THINK TANK

A few tricks of the road will keep the black and gray holding tanks in an RV odor-free and operating smoothly.

- **Use an Enzyme-Based Holding Tank Treatment.** Bacteria in the holding tank need air to break down waste. Otherwise, the bacteria begin feeding on the anaerobic sulfates in the waste, producing a foul odor—toxic and corrosive hydrogen sulfide gas. A biodegradable, enzyme-based product provides an energy source for the bacteria, eliminating the emission of hydrogen sulfide and breaking down waste and toilet tissue.
- **Use the Proper Toilet Paper.** You want toilet paper designed for RV waste systems or household toilet paper approved for septic tank use.
- **Avoid Using Excess Toilet Paper.** You know why.
- **Use Adequate Water for Flushing.** Otherwise, too little water in the black tank can inhibit drainage when dumping, resulting in undesirable buildup in the tank.
- **Clean Residue from a Black Tank.** Fill the tank with water, add a tank treatment or cleaner/degreaser (like Simple Green) and ice, and

drive around. The ice agitates the tank contents and cleans the residue from the tank walls.

- **Check the Roof.** If the tank odor persists, check to see whether the roof vent from the sewer system is obstructed by a bird's nest, beehive or wasp nest, or some other blockage.
- **Eliminate Gray Tank Odors.** If the gray tank and the plumbing leading to it emit odors, use the same enzyme-based treatments to clean it.
- **Have the Right Equipment.** Make sure you have a complete hose kit (a good-quality 10-to-20-foot sewer hose, firmly attached bayonet fittings, and a hose support system) for use at an RV park or dump station.
- **Avoid Disease.** Use latex medical gloves to protect yourself from contact with human waste (which carries disease) at the dump station.

OFF THE BEATEN TRACK

How to Find Free Overnight RV Parking

- **Be Presentable and Polite.** A clean, well-kept appearance and good manners make a favorable first impression and conveys your respect for the property of others.
- **Check Out Walmart and Other Stores.** Many Walmart locations across the country allow RVs to park overnight in the parking lot for free (without hookups for electricity, water, or dump stations). Find a directory of those locations at www.allstays.com/c/wal-mart -locations.htm. Double-check with the store manager to make sure camping is allowed, and confirm that the neighborhood is safe. Other businesses that allow RVs to spend the night in their parking lots include Camping World, Kmart, truck stops (including Travel Centers of America and Flying J), casinos, and supermarkets.
- **Join an Elks Club or Moose Lodge.** Members of the Elks or Moose can park at any Elks Club or Moose Lodge in the country for free.
- **Ask the Police.** Stop by the local police station and ask where you can park your RV for the night. By introducing yourself up front (rather than having an officer knock at your RV door late at night in a school or church parking lot), the police will identify you as a law-abiding citizen and may invite you to use their parking lot.
- **Ask Permission.** If you wish to park overnight on public or private property, ask for permission, and make sure you're not inconveniencing the property owner in any way.
- **Ask Locals.** In a small town, ask the personnel at the visitor center, the owner of a sporting goods store, the gas station attendant, or the manager of the grocery store where you might be able to park for free in a safe, secluded spot. Many small towns offer a free night's stay in the city park or campground (with free electrical hookups) to draw tourists to spend money in their business district.
- **Declare Your Intentions.** Explain that you need a place to park and sleep for just one night, and explain why you're traveling.
- **Avoid the Word *Camping*.** No one wants you setting up a tent, sitting around a campfire, or using the outdoors as your latrine. Insist that you'll spend the night quietly inside your RV, where you have your own bathroom.
- **Befriend Security Officers.** If you obtain permission to stay overnight in a parking lot for a store, casino, or public transit station, approach the security guards before they approach you. Tell them how long you'll be staying, explain what you'll be

doing, and offer the guards a cup of hot coffee. In return for your kindness, the officers will likely guard your RV.

- **Remain Inconspicuous.** Park along the curb, and keep the noise and the use of your interior lights to a minimum, and spend as little time in the RV as possible. Do not set up an awning, barbecue, or lawn furniture.
- **Do Not Overstay Your Welcome.** Stick to your agreed departure date and time so the property owner doesn't feel compelled to ask you to leave or call the authorities.
- **Seek Out Festivals.** During special festival weekends, towns and cities tend to offer free overnight RV parking in public parks and overflow camping areas near the festivities.
- **Consider the Parking Lot of a Bar.** Not wanting patrons to drink and drive, bartenders are accustomed to seeing a vehicle left in the parking lot overnight. Just be sure to leave first thing in the morning.
- **Never Argue.** If an authority figure tells you to vacate the area, apologize profusely, thank the person for informing you of the problem, and agree to leave. Ask the security guard or police officer to suggest a safe and lawful place nearby where you can park your RV overnight for free.
- **Show Your Appreciation.** Before leaving, thank your host profusely, and if possible, give a small gift to show your gratitude. Or send a postcard within a few days to say thank you.

How to Insulate Camper Windows with Bubble Wrap

WHAT YOU NEED
- Scissors
- Bubble Wrap
- Spray bottle
- Water
- Scotch tape or double-sided tape (optional)

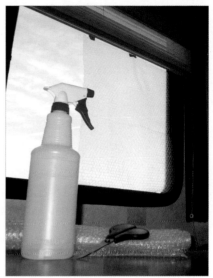

WHAT TO DO
1. Using scissors, carefully cut the Bubble Wrap to the size of the windowpane.
2. Fill the spray bottle with water, and spray a light film of water on the inside of the window.
3. Immediately apply the Bubble Wrap to the wet glass (with the bubble side facing toward the glass) and press it into place.
4. Smooth the sheet of Bubble Wrap against the glass so the water holds it in place.
5. Repeat for each window.
6. If the Bubble Wrap refuses to stick to the windows, use a few small strips of Scotch tape or double-sided tape to adhere the Bubble Wrap to the glass.
7. To remove the Bubble Wrap from the windows, simply start from a corner and pull it free. Neither Bubble Wrap nor water leaves any stains on the windows. Save the sheets of Bubble Wrap for reuse.

HOW IT WORKS
Bubble Wrap creates a radiant barrier of insulation, preventing heat from escaping the camper through the glass. The Bubble Wrap increases the R-value of a single-pane window from less than R1 to approximately R2, cutting the heat loss through the window in half. Using water to adhere the Bubble Wrap to the windows avoids the need for tape, which leaves adhesive residue on the glass.

DOUBLE BUBBLE

To increase the insulation, add a second layer of Bubble Wrap by cutting a second sheet to match the size of the first. Spray a mist of water on the first layer of Bubble Wrap, and immediately apply the second sheet (with the bubble side facing the glass), and smooth it into place.

KEEPING IT UNDER WRAPS

When you remove the sheets of Bubble Wrap from the windows, use an indelible marker to write a number on the upper right-hand corner of each sheet. On a piece of paper, draw a diagram of the trailer, numbering windows to correspond with the numbers on the sheets of Bubble Wrap.

OFF THE BEATEN TRACK

How to Get Better Gas Mileage in an RV

An RV gets fewer miles per gallon than a car, due to significant weight and increased wind resistance, but here's how to increase your fuel efficiency with a large motor home.

- Make sure you keep the engine tuned and the air filter clean and new. Clean air filters improve performance and fuel efficiency by up to 10 percent.
- Frequent oil changes (and synthetic oils) with the recommended grade increase fuel efficiency.
- Use cruise control when possible. Keeping the RV at a constant, rather than variable, speed—particularly when traveling around 60 MPH—saves gas.
- Avoid using the dashboard air conditioner unnecessarily. The air conditioner puts stress on the engine and reduces gas mileage.
- Empty the water and waste tanks before hitting the road. This lessens the weight you're carrying.
- Do not overload the RV. Excess weight requires more fuel.
- Keep the tires inflated to maximum pressure (or slightly under). Proper tire pressure increases your fuel economy by up to 3 percent.
- Keep your wheels balanced and make sure the brakes do not drag.
- Use the correct transmission fluid and maintain the proper level. Keep the automatic transmission adjusted to shift properly.
- Drive at slower speeds.
- Minimize the amount of time you allow the engine to idle.
- Utilize low transmission ranges less frequently.

How to Protect Wine Bottles with Beer Can Koozies

WHAT YOU NEED
- Beer can koozie

WHAT TO DO
1. Insert the base of the wine bottle into the beer can koozie.
2. Wedge the padded wine bottle between objects in a drawer or cabinet aboard the RV to prevent it from shifting.

HOW IT WORKS
The foam padding of the koozie helps protect the glass bottle from breaking.

EVERY TRICK IN THE BOOK
Getting Nice and Koozie

A few other uses for koozies:

- **Prevent Bruised Fruit.** Place an apple, orange, or pear inside a koozie before putting it in your backpack or bag.
- **Store Lightbulbs Safely.** To keep lightbulbs from shattering, carefully insert each lightbulb into a koozie.
- **Protect and Store a Camera Lens.** Insert the lens inside a foam koozie.
- **Prevent Rust Marks on the Bottom of a Shaving Cream Can.** Place the shaving cream can inside a koozie.
- **Store a Poster.** Roll up the poster, and place a koozie on each end of the tube to hold it in place.
- **Protect a Car Gearshift from the Sun's Heat.** Place a koozie over the stick.
- **Keep Your Hands Warm.** In a pinch, two koozies double as mittens.
- **Hold Pencils and Pens.** Use a koozie on your desk as a pencil holder.

How to Make a Garbage Can with a Collapsible Laundry Basket

WHAT YOU NEED
- Collapsible laundry basket
- Plastic trash bag

WHAT TO DO
1. Set up the collapsible laundry basket.
2. Insert the trash bag inside the laundry basket and fold the lip of the bag back over the mouth of the basket.
3. When you're packing up camp, remove the garbage bag and discard it.
4. Fold up the laundry basket and store it, or use it for its original purpose—as a hamper for dirty laundry.

HOW IT WORKS
The wire-frame collapsible laundry basket pops open and supports the weight not only of dirty laundry but of trash as well.

BASKET CASES
- In September 2014, Israeli performance artist Yoav Admoni disguised himself as a plant by binding fresh-cut reeds to a collapsible laundry hamper with a spool of wire. The artist waded 13 miles through canals from Tijuana, Mexico, to the United States as the third installment in his *A Threesome with Nature* thesis project for the Bauhaus University in Weimar, Germany.
- In 2012, the *Ann Arbor News* reported that special effects artist Dave Hettmer bought a green collapsible laundry hamper, sewed silver fabric onto the top and bottom, and added a red sash with the felt letters *S-O-D-A* sewed onto it—because his daughter wanted a soda can costume for Halloween one year.

How to Make a Tissue Box Dispenser with a Food Container

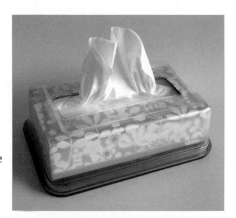

WHAT YOU NEED

- Low-profile tissue box
- Plastic potluck-size food storage container, 80 ounce
- Indelible marker
- Utility knife

WHAT TO DO

1. Remove the cardboard strip covering the slot in the top of the tissue box.
2. Place the bottom of the plastic container upside down over the tissue box.
3. Using the indelible marker, trace the perimeter of the slot onto the plastic.
4. Remove the tissue box, and using the utility knife, cut out the slot you traced in the bottom of the plastic container.
5. Place the tissue box upside down inside the container.
6. Seal the lid of the container.

HOW IT WORKS

The plastic box protects the cardboard tissue box from getting wet or crushed.

A NOSE FOR MARKETING

Kimberly-Clark Corporation began marketing Kleenex tissues in 1922 as a makeup remover for women. But people started writing to the company raving that the tissues doubled as disposable handkerchiefs. At first Kimberly-Clark executives didn't want people blowing their noses in their product, but they quickly realized that more people blow their noses than wear makeup.

How to Relieve Back or Neck Pain with Rice and a Sock

WHAT YOU NEED

- Sock
- Rice
- 3 chamomile tea bags (optional)
- Microwave oven

WHAT TO DO

1. Fill the sock with rice.
2. Remove the staples from the tea bags, and insert the tea bags into the sock with the rice, if desired.
3. Tie a knot in the open end of the sock.
4. Heat the rice-filled sock in a microwave oven for 90 seconds.
5. Apply the heated sock to the back of your neck, your forehead, knee, back, or wherever you're experiencing pain.
6. Reheat the rice-filled sock as needed.

HOW IT WORKS

The heated rice inside the sock works as a heating pad, conforming to the shape of your body and remaining hot for approximately 10 minutes. The chamomile tea provides soothing aromatherapy. The homemade heating pad is reusable.

EVERY TRICK IN THE BOOK

A Royal Pain

Here are a few other ways to reduce back and neck pain:

- **Bubble Wrap.** Cut rectangular sheets of Bubble Wrap and stuff them into an empty pillowcase or a gallon-size ziplock freezer bag. Place the pillow behind the small of your back when driving.
- **Green Peas.** Wrap a plastic bag of frozen green peas in a paper towel and use it as an ice pack for 10 minutes.
- **Mustard.** Rub regular yellow mustard over your back to allow the heat from the condiment to relieve the pain.

How to Deodorize a Microwave Oven with Lemon Juice

WHAT YOU NEED
- Lemon juice
- Coffee mug
- Water

WHAT TO DO
1. Pour 2 tablespoons of lemon juice in a coffee mug.
2. Fill the rest of the mug with water.
3. Heat the cup of lemon water in the microwave for 1 minute on the high setting.
4. Use a sponge to wipe down the inside of the microwave oven.

HOW IT WORKS
The steam from the lemony water infuses the inside of the microwave, deodorizing it.

MESSING AROUND
- To stop food from splattering on the walls and ceiling of the microwave oven when cooking, cover the food with a microwave safe lid, waxed paper, plastic wrap, or a paper towel during cooking. Do not use paper or other flammable materials to cover the food if you are using a heating element or browning dish to brown the food.
- Clean up spatters and spills when they happen. Use a damp cloth and mild soap. Do not use harsh detergents or abrasives. Continuing to use the microwave oven after food has been spattered inside the oven can cause the oven to work less efficiently and causes that food to bake into the floor, walls, or ceiling of the oven.
- To help loosen baked-on food particles or liquids, heat 2 cups of water (add the juice of one lemon if you desire to keep the oven fresh) in a 4-cup measuring glass at high power for 5 minutes or until boiling. Let it stand in the oven for 1 or 2 minutes. The resulting steam helps loosen baked-on food or liquids.
- Remove the glass tray when cleaning. To prevent the glass tray from breaking, handle it carefully and do not put the glass tray in water immediately after cooking. Wash the tray carefully in warm, sudsy water or in the dishwasher.

EVERY TRICK IN THE BOOK

Getting Fresh

Here are some other cool ways to deodorize a microwave oven:

- **Coffee Grounds.** Put 2 tablespoons of coffee grounds in a small bowl, place the bowl inside the unplugged microwave oven, shut the door, and let it sit overnight. The coffee grounds absorb smells as potent as burnt popcorn. Or mix 2 tablespoons of coffee grounds in a mug filled halfway with water, and cook it for 2 minutes on the high setting.
- **Vanilla Extract.** Pour 1 tablespoon of vanilla extract in a coffee mug, and cook it in the microwave for 30 seconds or more. Leave the microwave door shut overnight. In the morning, remove the coffee mug, and use a damp sponge to wipe down the inside of the microwave oven.
- **Vinegar.** To deodorize a smelly microwave oven, pour 1 cup of vinegar in a bowl, and cook it in the microwave oven for 5 minutes, allowing the vinegar to boil. The steam from the vinegar wafts through the fan mechanism, neutralizing the smells in the microwave oven.

How to Deodorize a Cooler with Vanilla Extract

WHAT YOU NEED

- ¾ cup bleach
- Hot water
- Sponge
- Vanilla extract

WHAT TO DO

1. Mix ¾ cup of bleach and 1 gallon of hot water.
2. Using a sponge, wash the inside of the cooler with the solution.
3. Rinse the cooler clean with water, and let it air dry with the lid open.
4. Saturate the sponge with vanilla extract and wipe down the insides.
5. Let the cooler, coated with vanilla extract, air dry with the lid open.

HOW IT WORKS

The bleach sanitizes the inside of the cooler, and the vanilla extract masks any lingering smells.

EVERY TRICK IN THE BOOK

Come Out Smelling like a Rose

Here are a few more ways to neutralize odors with vanilla extract:

- **Deodorize a Refrigerator.** Dampen a cotton ball with vanilla extract, and place it on a saucer in your refrigerator to neutralize odors.
- **Freshen Musty Rooms.** Saturate a cotton ball with vanilla extract, place it on a saucer, and set the saucer in a musty basement, bathroom, or closet.
- **Deodorize Paint Fumes.** Before painting interior walls, mix 1 tablespoon of vanilla extract into a gallon of paint.
- **Deodorize Your Home.** Before vacuuming, dab your vacuum cleaner filter with a few drops of vanilla extract to infuse your carpet with the pleasant aroma.
- **Freshen the Air in Your Home.** Before turning on the lights (when the bulbs are cool to the touch), smear 1 or 2 drops of vanilla extract on the glass lightbulbs. When turned on, the bulbs will warm the vanilla and send the scent wafting through your home.

How to Prevent Ice on a Windshield with Vinegar

WHAT YOU NEED

- Vinegar
- Water
- 16-ounce trigger-spray bottle

WHAT TO DO

1. To avoid getting an icy car windshield overnight, mix 12 ounces of vinegar and 4 ounces of water in a 16-ounce trigger-spray bottle.
2. Spray the glass with the solution.

HOW IT WORKS

The thin coat of vinegar solution freezes to the glass before the rain or frost does, preventing ice from forming.

CHILL OUT

- Household hints newspaper columnist Heloise advocated this idea in 1980: "Vinegar also helps retard frost on those cold mornings if you pour it on the windshield the night before (three parts cider vinegar to one part water)."
- Some people caution that vinegar sprayed on the windshield will pit the glass. This claim is false. Vinegar is sold in glass bottles, and the weak acetic acid does not pit that glass, nor will it harm a windshield.
- To avoid scraping ice off your windshield, use scissors to cut a broad sheet of plastic from a clean, used shower curtain to cover the windshield and overhang each side. Place the plastic sheet over the windshield, and close the car doors over the edges of the plastic to hold it in place. When you're ready to drive, brush off any snow and peel off the plastic for an ice-free windshield. To make a more elaborate windshield cover, use a sewing machine to hem the plastic with strong magnets inside the hems.
- If you don't have a shower curtain, cut open a large plastic trash bag, place it over the entire windshield, and close the car doors over the edges of the bag to hold it in place.

How to Make a Portable Trash Can with a Plastic Cereal Container

WHAT YOU NEED

- Small plastic bag
- Plastic cereal container

WHAT TO DO

1. Place a small plastic bag inside the cereal container as a liner, folding the top of the plastic bag over the edge of the container.
2. Snap the cover in place.
3. Pop open the flip top, shove your trash inside, and seal the flip top shut.
4. Store the homemade trash can on the floor in front of the passenger seat.

HOW IT WORKS

The small container stores trash conveniently and compactly, the flip top prevents trash from falling out, and the container takes up little space in your vehicle.

EVERY TRICK IN THE BOOK

How Do You Contain Your Enthusiasm?

- **Diaper Hamper.** A cereal container lined with a trash bag makes an excellent travel hamper for dirty disposable diapers.
- **Hamster House.** Remove the flip top, place the cereal container inside the habitat, and the hamster will climb inside the transparent container. Or to give a rodent inhaler treatments for respiratory distress, place treats inside the container, and when the animal climbs inside, spray the inhaler through the opening, and close the flip top for a few minutes.
- **Pet Food Dispenser.** Store pet food inside a cereal container for easy dispensing. Just make sure to label the container so family members do not mistake cat food for some sort of snack.

How to Trigger a Broken Gas Pump Handle with a Tennis Ball

WHAT YOU NEED
- Tennis ball

WHAT TO DO
1. If the hold-open clip or clamp is missing or broken from the handle of a gas pump, insert the nozzle into the gas tank.
2. Activate the trigger and wedge a tennis ball between the trigger and the handle.

HOW IT WORKS
The tennis ball, jammed between the handle and the trigger, blocks the gas pump open, so you don't have to hold the gas pump and inhale the gas fumes.

RUNNING ON EMPTY
- ***Perform this travel secret at your own risk:*** if the pump gets jostled or if gasoline backs up from the gas tank with any force, the tennis ball may not jar free—allowing gas to gush from the nozzle.
- Never use a tennis ball to prop open a gas nozzle when filling a gas can for a lawnmower or snowblower. The weight of the nozzle will likely tip over the entire gas can.
- In 2013, police arrested Neal Grubbs, 20, for plotting to blow up movie theaters in Indianapolis with "tennis ball bombs"—a tennis ball filled with BBs and capped with a fuse.

8

CAMPING

Having paid for a campsite in the Australian outback during a torrential rainstorm, I insisted on pitching our tent on the prescribed raised wooden platform—while Debbie sat in the car. Despite my dogged determination, fierce winds kept blowing the tent away, thwarting my repeated efforts to stake it down. Sopping wet, I reluctantly heeded Debbie's pleas and conceded defeat. Now where would we stay? At Debbie's suggestion, we set up our tent in the campsite restroom.

How to Make a Barbecue Grill from a Coffee Can and a Rake

WHAT YOU NEED

- Tin snips
- Clean, empty coffee can
- Small rocks or gravel
- Aluminum foil
- Charcoal
- Butane lighter or matches
- Steel leaf rake

WHAT TO DO

1. Using tin snips, carefully cut 12 vertical slats (like around the face of a clock) from the top of the can down to 1 inch from the bottom of the can.

2. Fold back the slats to create the wings of a fan in a bowl-like shape.

3. Place small rocks or gravel in the empty base of the can (to weight it down and prevent the stove from toppling over).

4. Cover the bowl with a sheet of aluminum foil.

5. Place the coffee can on a flat surface, and fill the aluminum bowl with charcoal.

6. After igniting the charcoal, place the rake over the mouth of the bowl to create the grill.

HOW IT WORKS

The tines of the steel leaf rake form the grill, and the coffee can forms the frame of a barbecue pan, created by the aluminum foil, to hold the charcoal.

ALL FIRED UP

- In the 17th century, Spanish explorers in Hispaniola discovered that the native Arawak tribe slow-cooked meat on a frame of sticks over a fire, calling it *barbacòa*. The Spanish adopted the method.
- In 1897, Ellsworth B. A. Zwoyer of Pennsylvania patented a design for charcoal briquettes.
- In 1952, George Stephen, a welder at Weber Brothers Metal Works in Chicago, cut a metal buoy in half to make a dome-shaped grill, using the top half as a lid, and added some air vents and legs, giving birth to the iconic Weber grill.

How to Keep a Bar of Soap Clean with Panty Hose

WHAT YOU NEED

- Scissors
- Pair of clean, used panty hose
- Bar of soap

WHAT TO DO

1. Using a pair of scissors, carefully cut off one leg from a clean, used pair of panty hose.
2. Drop a bar of soap in the panty hose leg.
3. Tie a knot to secure the bar of soap in the foot.
4. Tie the other end of the leg to an outdoor water spigot or tree branch.

HOW IT WORKS

The panty hose keeps the bar of soap clean and accessible.

CLEAN AS A WHISTLE

- Prior to the introduction of modern hygiene in the 19th century, the human body was often infected with parasites that transmitted typhus, bubonic plague, and many other illnesses.
- Body odor is caused not by perspiration itself but by bacteria on the skin's surface breaking down the perspiration. Left uncleansed, the skin becomes a breeding ground for germs.
- According to the Mayo Clinic, washing your hands frequently and thoroughly with soap and water for at least 15 seconds (or using an alcohol-based hand sanitizer) helps you avoid getting and spreading the flu.

EVERY TRICK IN THE BOOK

Panty Hose to the Rescue

You can also use panty hose for these purposes:

- **Back Scrubber.** Cut off the leg of a pair of used panty hose, stick a bar of soap inside at the knee, tie a knot around both ends, and use the panty hose to wash your back.
- **Cactus Spine Remover.** To remove thin, hairlike cactus spines from the skin, put on a pair of rubber gloves, and brush the affected area with a balled-up pair of clean, used panty hose in the opposite direction that the cactus spine went into the skin. The panty hose removes the needles, which adhere to the nylon hose. Discard the panty hose and gloves.
- **Cheese Strainer.** Boil a pair of clean, used panty hose in water, let it cool, and use it to strain cheese before pressing.
- **Fishing Lures.** Cut strips of used panty hose to make fishing lures.
- **Lint Catcher.** Cut off the foot of an old pair of panty hose and attach it to the end of the washer hose to catch all lint as it comes out, preventing the drain and pipes from clogging.
- **Nail Polish Remover.** Ball up a pair of used, clean panty hose, add a drop of nail polish remover, and scrub your nails. The polish comes off with ease.
- **Onion Storage.** Cut off the legs from a used, clean pair of panty hose, insert one onion down to the bottom, tie a knot after it, and repeat until you either run out of onions or panty hose leg. Then hang up the panty hose leg.
- **Pot Scrubber.** Place a used pair of panty hose in a webbed onion bag from the grocery store to make an excellent pot scrubber.
- **Shoe Shine Cloth.** Cut the legs from a pair of clean, used panty hose to put a lustrous shine on shoes.
- **Tomato Plant Supports.** Cut 1-inch strips of panty hose and use them as ties to support plants and vegetables on stakes. The strips are like firm elastic that stretches as the plant grows.

How to Lubricate Zippers on a Sleeping Bag and Tent with Lip Balm

WHAT YOU NEED

- Lip balm
- Soft cloth or paper towel (optional)

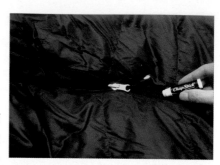

WHAT TO DO

1. Rub lip balm along the teeth of the zipper on the sleeping bag or tent (or trousers, jackets, and backpacks), over the entire length of the zipper. Do not rub the lip balm on the fabric, just the metal or plastic zipper parts. If the zipper is stuck, rub the lip balm on the teeth above and below the stuck slide.

2. Jiggle the slide until it moves freely over the waxed teeth. Slowly move the slide back and forth along the teeth, zipping and unzipping several times. This action helps work the wax through the teeth.

3. Brush off any excess wax with your fingers, a soft cloth, or a paper towel.

HOW IT WORKS

The wax in the lip balm lubricates the teeth, helping the zipper zip smoothly.

ADD SOME ZIP

- Other lubricants you can rub along the teeth of a stubborn zipper to make it glide with greater ease include petroleum jelly, vegetable shortening, a dry bar of soap, a candle, a sheet of waxed paper, an unwrapped crayon, and the graphite of a dull pencil.
- To prevent a zipper from unzipping of its own accord, spray the teeth with hair spray or spray starch to give them greater traction.

How to Make a Camping Sink with a Bleach Bottle

WHAT YOU NEED

- Ice pick
- Clean, empty bleach bottle
- Golf tee
- Length of string or yarn, 2 feet long
- Water
- Rope (optional)
- Indelible markers (optional)
- Plastic bucket (optional)

WHAT TO DO

1. Use the ice pick to poke a small hole near the bottom of the bleach bottle on the side opposite the handle.
2. Plug the hole with the pointed end of the golf tee.
3. Use a piece of string or yarn to tie the tee to the handle.
4. You can also slip a bar of soap in a panty hose leg and tie it to the handle, if desired (see page 190).
5. Fill the bottle with water, replace the cap, and set it on the edge of a picnic table, upright log, or rock. Or tie a piece of rope around the handle and hang the jug from a post or tree branch.
6. Use the indelible markers to decorate the bottle with lips around the hole, and eyes, nose, ears, and hair above to turn the jug into a spitting face.
7. If desired, place a bucket under the spout to catch the water to avoid creating a mud hole.
8. To wash your hands, loosen the cap and unplug the golf tee.
9. When you're finished, replace the tee in the hole and tighten the cap.

HOW IT WORKS

The string prevents the tee from getting lost. When the cap is loosened and the tee is removed, air pressure pushes down and up through both openings, so the air pressure is balanced. Gravity makes the water fall from the jug through the smaller hole. When the cap is tightened, the air pressure can only push from the bottom. The air pressure is stronger than earth's gravity, so it keeps the water in the jug.

EVERY TRICK IN THE BOOK

Hitting the Bottle

Here are a few more things you can do with a bleach bottle:

- **Drill Holster.** To make a hip holster for carrying a drill, cut off the bottom of an empty, clean, uncapped bleach bottle in a diagonal opposite the handle, and then string your belt through the handle.
- **Dumbbells.** Fill two clean, empty bleach bottles with water, sand, or gravel, seal the caps shut, and use the handles to lift the weights.
- **Funnel.** Use a pair of sharp scissors to cut off the bottom of a bleach bottle to create a funnel with a convenient handle.
- **Scooper.** Use a pair of sharp scissors to cut diagonally across the middle of an empty, clean bleach bottle, and use the half with the handle to scoop up pet food, fertilizer, rock salt, sugar, or snow, or to clean up after your pet.
- **Tool Caddy.** Use a utility knife to cut a hole in the side opposite the handle of a clean, empty bleach bottle to carry tools.
- **Watering Can.** Use an ice pick or awl to punch holes in the cap, fill the clean, empty bottle with water, and replace the cap. Holding the handle, use the water-filled jug as a watering can.
- **Weights.** Clean, empty bleach bottles filled with water, sand, or gravel and capped shut can be used to hold down a tarp or tent.

How to Make a Portable Shower with a Condom

WHAT YOU NEED
- Condom
- Scissors
- Pair of clean, used panty hose
- Safety pin, needle, or pin

WHAT TO DO
1. Unwrap the condom, unravel it, and fill it with water, like a water balloon.
2. Tie a knot in the open end of the condom.
3. Using the scissors, snip off one leg from the pair of panty hose.
4. Slip the water-filled condom inside the panty hose leg, with the reservoir tip facing the toe.
5. Toss the free end of the panty hose leg over a tall, solid tree branch, and hoist the water-filled condom approximately 6 feet off the ground.

6. Tie the free end of the panty hose leg to the trunk of the tree or a low branch to secure the water-filled condom in place.
7. Gather your soap and towel, and remove your clothes (or put on a bathing suit).
8. Pinch the reservoir tip of the condom and, using the safety pin, needle, or pin, puncture a few small holes in the tip.
9. Stand under the stream of water to take your shower.

HOW IT WORKS
The latex rubber used to make the condom is sufficiently durable and elastic to hold water. The nylon stocking prevents the weight of the water from bursting the condom, and the contraction of the condom's surface forces the water from the holes to create a strong spray.

CONDOM CONUNDRUMS

- Drug smuggling mules have been known to swallow condoms filled with heroin or cocaine to evade detection by customs officials. They take medications to inhibit bowel movements during the journey, and use laxatives at their destination to pass the balloons through their bodies. If stomach acids or other incidents rupture a balloon inside the body, the consequence is quick death.
- In July 2014, an Englishman from Birmingham who had swallowed 61 latex condoms of cocaine before boarding a Virgin Atlantic flight from Antigua to London sparked an emergency landing when one of the packs burst in his stomach. Colmin Smith, 48, informed a flight attendant about what he had done and then lost consciousness. The plane landed in Bermuda, where doctors removed 8.4 ounces of cocaine from Smith's stomach.
- On February 6, 2011, police arrested Luisa Gill, 21, at Boston's Logan Airport with 50 latex condoms of cocaine stored in her stomach. Gill, a resident of New Jersey, swallowed nearly a pound of cocaine—with an estimated street value of $50,000—before boarding a JetBlue flight from the Dominican Republic.

EVERY TRICK IN THE BOOK
More Clever Uses for Condoms

- **Cell Phone Protector.** To improvise a waterproof case for your cell phone, slip the device inside an unlubricated condom.
- **Ice Pack.** Fill a condom with water, like a water balloon, tie a knot in the open end, and place it in the freezer to create an emergency ice pack.
- **Match Container.** A condom doubles as a waterproof container for matches.
- **Slingshot.** Construct a slingshot from a Y-shaped tree branch and a condom.
- **Stress Ball.** Fill a condom with sand or flour, and tie a knot in the open end.
- **Tourniquet.** Tying a condom around a bleeding appendage works as a tourniquet.
- **Water Carrier.** Place the condom inside a sock, fill the condom with water, and tie a knot in the open end of the condom. The sock provides stability and protection.

How to Waterproof a Backpack with a Trash Bag

WHAT YOU NEED

- 2 heavy-duty plastic trash bags (the size of your backpack)
- Scissors or pocketknife

WHAT TO DO

1. Line the inside of the backpack with a plastic trash bag.
2. Pack your clothes and gear inside the trash bag.
3. Zip up the backpack.
4. Place the second trash bag over the backpack.
5. Use the scissors or pocketknife to carefully cut small slits in the bag for the straps.
6. Pull the straps through the slits.
7. Pull the drawstring tightly shut at the bottom of the backpack.

HOW IT WORKS

Most backpacks are not waterproof. Even those made from waterproof fabrics generally have porous seams. Heavy-duty plastic trash bags are tough, durable, and waterproof—protecting your clothes and gear from rain and wet surfaces.

HIGH AND DRY

- Double bagging (lining one bag inside the other) doubles the effectiveness of the bags, since plastic trash bags can get punctured easily.
- Experienced hikers often prefer using trash compactor bags, which are smaller, narrower, and thicker than commercial trash bags.
- Plastic trash bags make poor waterproofing for your gear on canoeing or rafting trips. Plastic bags easily get puncture holes, which let water—from splashes, capsizing, or the puddle on the bottom of a wet canoe, kayak, or raft—seep inside. Instead, use a waterproof dry sack with a roll-top closure.

How to Repair a Tent or Backpack with Dental Floss

WHAT YOU NEED

- Scissors or sharp pocketknife
- Waxed dental floss
- Needle (with large enough opening for dental floss)
- Isopropyl alcohol pads or baby wipes
- Seam sealer

WHAT TO DO

Punctures

1. To repair a hole poked through the tent fabric, use scissors or a sharp pocketknife to carefully cut away the damaged area and leave enough of the tent fabric to create tabs that you can fold back to create a hemmed frame.
2. Use scissors or a sharp pocketknife to cut a small patch of the same material.
3. Fold back each side of the patch to prevent the fabric from fraying, and using a needle threaded with waxed dental floss, sew the patch to the outside surface of the damaged area.
4. Clean the patch, seams, and surrounding area with isopropyl alcohol pads or baby wipes.
5. Seal the seams of the patch with seam sealer to avoid leakage.

Tears

1. To patch a rip in the fabric or a tear in a seam line, lay a wide piece of fabric or ribbon over the split.
2. Fold back each side of the patch to prevent the fabric from fraying, and using a needle threaded with dental floss, sew the fabric or ribbon onto the adjacent fabric to disperse the tension away from the seam.

HOW IT WORKS

Waxed dental floss is far more durable than thread.

EVERY TRICK IN THE BOOK

Why Floss Is Boss

Some great uses for dental floss when traveling:

- **Repair Eyeglasses.** If the screw from the hinge of your eyeglasses is lost, tie a piece of dental floss through the screw holes for a temporary repair until you can get the glasses fixed properly.
- **Repair an Umbrella.** If one of the fabric tacks breaks free from one of the ribs of an umbrella, sew it back together using dental floss as a durable thread.
- **Sew Buttons on Coats.** Use dental floss as a strong, durable substitute for thread to sew on buttons on coats and children's clothes.
- **Cut Clean Slices of Cake.** Hold a strand of dental floss as if you were going to floss your teeth, and cut through the cake.
- **Cut Cheese into Clean Slices.** Hold a strand of dental floss as if you were going to floss your teeth, and cut through the cheese.
- **Lift Cookies from a Cookie Sheet with Ease.** Slide a strand of dental floss between fresh baked cookies and the cookie sheet.
- **Cut Cookie or Bun Roll Dough into Neat Slices.** Slide a strand of dental floss under the roll, cross the two ends over the top of the roll, and pull.
- **Truss Poultry.** Use durable dental floss to tie the legs together and sew up the cavity. Dental floss is more durable than thread and won't tear the skin.
- **Slice Cheesecake.** To cut a cheesecake into neat, clean slices, use the technique embraced by fancy restaurants everywhere. Cut a strand of dental floss a few inches longer than the diameter of the cake. Hold the ends of the strand in each hand, making the floss taut, and press the string down to cut the cake in half. Slide the floss out from under the bottom of the cake, and repeat the process, cutting the cake into clean slices.
- **Dry Mushrooms.** Wash the mushrooms quickly, cut them in half lengthwise, and using a large needle and dental floss, string them together, leaving an inch between each mushroom half, and hang them outdoors for two days or until they are completely dry. Store the mushrooms in an airtight container on the pantry shelf. Rehydrate dried mushrooms by soaking them in water, chicken stock, or beef stock for 1 hour.

- **Remove a Wart from a Horse's Hide.** Tie off the wart tightly with a piece of dental floss. The dental floss will strangulate the wart, causing it to fall off after roughly a week, typically without leaving a scar.
- **String a Beaded Necklace or Bracelet.** Cut a piece of dental floss the length you desire for a necklace or bracelet, tie one end loosely, but securely, to one bead (to prevent the other beads from falling off the string), then thread the other end of the floss through the beads. The sturdiness of the waxed floss enables you to thread the beads without using a needle. After threading all the beads, remove the stopper bead, and tie the two ends together.
- **Suture a Wound.** In an emergency situation, you can use a sterile needle and unwaxed dental floss to stitch a wound temporarily until you reach a hospital.

How to Wash Your Clothes with a Salad Spinner

WHAT YOU NEED

- Salad spinner
- Water
- Laundry detergent (or shampoo)

WHAT TO DO

1. Place the salad spinner in the sink and remove the lid.
2. Begin filling the bowl (with the basket inserted) with whatever temperature water you prefer.
3. While filling the bowl with water, add a squirt of laundry detergent.
4. Place a few garments in the salad spinner, submerging them in the soapy water, and knead them with your fingers for a minute.
5. Let the garments soak undisturbed for 5 minutes.
6. Lift the basket of clothes from the bowl, and pour the soapy water from the bowl down the drain.
7. Replace the basket of clothes in the empty bowl, and fill the bowl with fresh water, while kneading the garments.
8. Let the garments soak for 2 minutes.
9. Repeat steps 6 through 8 for a second rinse, or until the water is no longer soapy.
10. Lift the basket of clothes from the bowl, and dump the water down the drain.
11. Place the basket of clothes in the bowl, place the lid on the salad spinner, and pull the cord or turn the handle five times.
12. Stop the salad spinner, remove the cover, take out the basket of clothes, and pour out the water.
13. Repeat steps 11 and 12 several times, until you're satisfied that no more water remains in the garments.
14. Hang up the garments to drip dry.

HOW IT WORKS

The salad spinner uses centrifugal force to extract the rinse water from the clothes—far more effectively than wringing the water from the clothes by hand.

GOING FOR A SPIN

- Operating the salad spinner in the sink prevents the device from flying off a countertop or spraying water everywhere.

EVERY TRICK IN THE BOOK

Spin Doctors

A salad spinner can be used for much more than drying lettuce leaves:

- **Clean Broccoli or Cauliflower.** Cut up broccoli and cauliflower, soak the pieces in the spinner, and then spin them dry.
- **Clean Leeks.** Cut the leeks in half. Place the basket in the bowl, fill the basket with the leeks, add water, and let them soak. Lift out the basket to drain the water. Repeat if necessary, and then spin the leeks dry.
- **Remove Seeds from Canned Tomatoes.** Empty a can of whole tomatoes into the spinner, break them apart with your fingers, and spin them gently to let centrifugal force remove the seeds.
- **Rinse and Drain Beans.** Place canned beans in the basket, rinse them with water, and then spin them gently to remove the excess water.
- **Spin Excess Water from Pasta.** When making pasta salad or casseroles, use the salad spinner to spin the excess water out of the pasta, so your pasta salad isn't water.
- **Wash Berries.** Place the basket in the bowl, fill the basket with berries, add water, and let it sit for 3 minutes. Lift out the basket to drain the water without bruising the berries.
- **Wring Out a Swimsuit.** Place the swimsuit in the spinner, spin the excess water out of the garment, and then hang it up to dry.

How to Keep Toilet Paper Dry with a CD Spindle

CARRIER

WHAT YOU NEED
- Clean, empty 100-CD spindle with lid
- Roll of toilet paper
- Masking tape

WHAT TO DO
1. Remove the cover from the CD spindle.
2. Place the roll of toilet paper over the spindle.
3. Replace the lid and twist it shut.
4. When traveling, use a piece of masking tape to secure the lid to the bottom of the base.
5. To use, simply remove the tape, twist open the lid, and lift.

DISPENSER

WHAT YOU NEED
- Utility knife
- Clean, empty 100-CD spindle with lid
- Roll of toilet paper

WHAT TO DO
1. sing a utility knife, carefully cut out the inner circle of plastic from the top of the plastic lid.
2. Remove the cardboard tube from the center of the roll of toilet paper.
3. Feed the inner end of the toilet paper into the plastic lid and through the hole in the top.
4. Place the role of toilet paper over the spindle.
5. Replace the lid and twist it shut.
6. To use, pull the free end of the toilet paper.

HOW IT WORKS

With the carrier, the masking tape keeps the CD spindle securely shut while traveling in a vehicle. When you set up camp, the plastic lid and base keep the toilet paper protected and dry. With a few additional modifications, the spindle can also serve as a toilet paper dispenser.

DON'T FOLD, SPINDLE, OR MUTILATE

- A roll of toilet paper fits into a clean, empty coffee can, giving new meaning to the slogan "Good to the last drop."
- To store multiple rolls of toilet paper, make a post by adhering a clean plunger to the floor (simply press down the giant suction cup firmly), and then place several rolls over the stick.

EVERY TRICK IN THE BOOK
Rekindle That Spindle

- **Bagel Sandwich Container.** Insert the spindle through the hole in the center of your bagel sandwich, seal the lid shut, and carry it in your lunchbox.
- **Cell Phone Stand.** Use the base alone as the perfect stand by leaning your cell phone against the spindle.
- **Coin Box.** Use a utility knife to cut the inner circle from the plastic lid, and drop coins inside.
- **Cord Storage.** Wrap your cords around the spindle and replace the lid.
- **Hamster Wheel.** Use an ice pick to punch holes in the sides and top of the plastic lid, place a hamster or mouse inside the lid, carefully insert the spindle, and twist it shut. Secure the halves in place with a strip of masking tape, and then place the case on the floor on its side.
- **Tape Storage Container.** Drop rolls of masking tape, duct tape, and electrical tape over the spindle and replace the lid.
- **Pencil Holder.** Turn the lid upside down and store your pens and pencils inside.
- **Ribbon Organizer.** Place your spools of ribbon over the spindle and cover them with the lid.
- **Yarn Holder.** Punch a hole in the top of the lid, place a spool of yarn over the spindle, run the free end of the yard through the hole, and secure the lid in place.

How to Make a Coffee Bag from Coffee Filters and Dental Floss

WHAT YOU NEED
- Coffee filter
- Fresh coffee grounds
- Dental floss
- Scissors

WHAT TO DO
1. Place a coffee filter on a flat working surface.
2. Spoon two or three teaspoons of fresh coffee grounds into the center of the coffee filter.
3. Gather the outer edges of the coffee filter to create a sachet.
4. Tie a loop of dental floss around the edge of the sachet and tie a secure knot or two.
5. Using scissors, trim the coffee filter beyond 1 inch of the tie.
6. Store the individual coffee bags in a ziplock bag.
7. To make a fresh cup of coffee, place a bag in a coffee cup, holding the floss outside the cup.
8. Fill the cup with boiling water.
9. Let it brew for several minutes, using the floss to dunk the coffee bag up and down.
10. Raise the floss to remove the coffee bag from the cup.

HOW IT WORKS
Pouring water heated to 200° Fahrenheit over ground coffee beans extracts the oil from the beans. The coffee filter contains the loose grounds and eliminates sediment.

YOUR CUP RUNNETH OVER

- Instead of using dental floss, you can also secure the coffee filter with a twist tie, and then dunk the bag in a cupful of boiling water with a spoon.
- To make Turkish coffee, boil 1 to 2 tablespoons of ground coffee in a pot, pour the solution into a coffee mug, and let the grounds settle to the bottom of the cup, and drink, stopping before you get to the mud at the bottom of the cup.
- To flavor coffee with cinnamon or vanilla, add a pinch of ground cinnamon or a few drops of vanilla extract to the coffee grounds before brewing.
- To improve the flavor of coffee, fill the coffee filter with the proper amount of ground coffee, add a pinch of salt to the coffee grounds, and brew as usual. The salt enhances the flavor.
- To remove the bitter taste from a cup of overheated coffee, add a pinch of salt to the cup of coffee and stir well.
- If you're all out of sugar or wish to try a more delectable sweetener for your coffee, use honey.
- You can flush coffee residue from a coffee grinder and simultaneously sharpen the blades by simply running one cup of rice through the grinder.

How to Hide Valuables in a Bar of Soap

WHAT YOU NEED

- Sharp knife or pocketknife
- Bar of soap
- Plastic wrap
- Water

WHAT TO DO

1. Using a sharp knife or pocketknife, carefully carve a cavity in a bar of soap.
2. Wrap the valuable item in a piece of plastic wrap, and insert the object inside the hollow.
3. Pack the hole with chunks and shavings of soap and press firmly to seal the hole.
4. Wet your fingertips with water and rub the veneer to smooth the appearance of the soap.

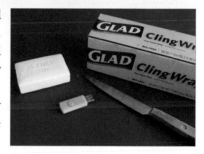

HOW IT WORKS

A knife easily carves soap, creating a secret compartment. The best place to hide a valuable item is in a common, everyday object that does not seem to provide any possibility as a hiding place.

How to Start a Charcoal Fire with an Egg Carton

WHAT YOU NEED
- Cardboard egg carton (not Styrofoam)
- 12 charcoal briquettes
- Butane lighter or matches

WHAT TO DO
1. Open the egg carton.
2. Place one charcoal briquette in each of the 12 compartments made for the eggs.
3. Close the egg carton lid.
4. Using the butane lighter or matches, ignite the cardboard egg carton.
5. Once the briquettes ignite, add more wood to the fire or more briquettes to the barbecue.

HOW IT WORKS
The cardboard egg carton burns long and strong enough to ignite the charcoal briquettes.

I AM THE EGG MAN
- Gardeners use egg cartons to start seedlings indoors in early spring, before planting the seedlings outdoors.
- Dirty or cracked eggs may transfer salmonella to their carton, where the bacteria can survive for weeks. ***Do not use cardboard cartons from untreated eggs*** for craft projects, storage, packing material, or other household uses where they will be handled regularly or come into contact with food. Repurposing cartons from eggs that have been treated to safeguard against salmonella contamination does not pose any risk of salmonellosis.
- In 2014, the Israeli Ministry of Health warned against the use of used egg cartons in kindergartens, day care centers, educational institutions, rehabilitation centers, and other institutions due to the risk of the presence of salmonella on the cartons.

How to Make Fire Starters with an Egg Carton and Dryer Lint

WHAT YOU NEED

- Cardboard egg carton (not Styrofoam)
- Dryer lint
- Candle
- Butane lighter or matches

WHAT TO DO

1. Open the egg carton.
2. Place dryer lint in each of the 12 compartments made for the eggs.
3. Light the candle and carefully drip hot wax over each compartment
4. Close the lid of the egg carton to transport the fire starters to your campsite.
5. To start the campfire, open the carton, tear off one of the compartments, and use it as kindling for your fire.

HOW IT WORKS

The paraffin-saturated lint burns long and strong enough to start a campfire.

LINT HINTS

- Lint is the short, fine fibers that separate from the surface of cloth during washing.
- The Consumer Product Safety Commission reports that lint buildup in the dryer or in the exhaust duct can cause fires. Lint can block the flow of air, cause overheating, and result in a fire in some dryers.
- To help prevent fires, consumers who use dryers should:
  » Clean the lint screen before or after drying each load of clothes.
  » Clean the dryer vent and exhaust duct periodically.

» Clean behind the dryer, where lint can build up.
» Replace plastic or foil, accordion-type ducting material with rigid or corrugated semi-rigid metal duct.
» Take special care when drying clothes that have been soiled with volatile chemicals.

How to Avoid Hypothermia with a Space Blanket

WHAT YOU NEED

- Hat
- Scarf (or cloth)
- Towel
- Dry clothes
- Space blanket
- Blanket
- Aluminum foil (optional)

WHAT TO DO

1. If a person's body temperature drops below 95° Fahrenheit, cover the person's head with a hat and wrap the neck with a scarf to slow the loss of heat from the head.
2. If possible, move the victim inside a warm, dry shelter.
3. Remove any wet clothes from the person and pat the skin dry with a towel.
4. If the victim is conscious, dress the individual in dry clothes.
5. Wrap the clothed body in a space blanket with the shiny side facing the body. For better effectiveness, wrap the body in a regular blanket and then wrap the space blanket around the blanket.
6. If you wish to have the victim lie down, place a layer of aluminum foil under a blanket or sleeping bag, and have the victim lie on top of that. This helps reflect body heat to keep the victim warmer.
7. If possible position the person to sit or lay by a warm fireplace or heater.

HOW IT WORKS

Excessive body heat loss leads to hypothermia, but wrapping the body in a space blanket reflects body heat back to the body and stops both evaporative and convective heat loss.

When a person perspires in cold weather, the perspiration evaporates, making the body colder. The space blanket helps slow the process of evaporative heat loss by increasing the humidity of the air next to the skin. In convective heat loss, cold wind takes the warmth away from the body. Wearing a layer of space blanket as insulation reduces convective heat loss by providing insulation.

COLD COMFORT

- Hypothermia occurs when the body temperature drops to below 95° Fahrenheit.
- When the body temperature drops, the body begins to shiver to produce body heat. If the body gets colder, the shivering ceases.
- Hypothermia can lead to loss of consciousness. If the victim is left untreated, breathing slows, the heart stops pumping blood, and death results.
- Falling through the ice of a frozen lake or river, taking a plunge into cold water, or getting soaking wet in a rainstorm could cause hypothermia.
- To thwart hypothermia, have the victim drink warm water sweetened with sugar, which quickly gives the body a source of energy to help warm the core. Aerobic activity—such as running in place or doing jumping jacks—also helps generate warmth.

How to Make a Spoon from a Soda Bottle

WHAT YOU NEED

- Indelible marker
- Clean, empty 2-liter plastic soda bottle
- Scissors or utility knife

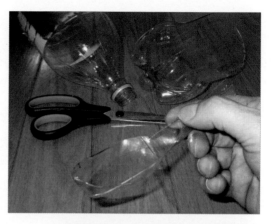

WHAT TO DO

1. Use the indelible marker to draw a pattern for the spoon on the outside of the plastic soda bottle. Draw an oblong oval around one nub on the bottom of the bottle (to create the bowl of the spoon), and from the top portion of the oval, draw a vertical rectangle (to create the handle of the spoon).

2. With the scissors or utility knife, carefully cut out the shape from the bottle.
3. Fold the handle of the spoon in half lengthwise.
4. Repeat the three steps above to make up to five spoons from one 2-liter bottle.

HOW IT WORKS

The nub of the bottle forms the bowl of the spoon, and folding the handle in half lengthwise increases the strength of the utensil.

WASTE NOT, WANT NOT

Rather than discarding the top half of the plastic bottle, save it for use as a funnel.

How to Store Spices in Tic Tac Boxes

WHAT YOU NEED

- Clean, empty Tic Tac boxes
- Spices
- Indelible marker
- Ziplock freezer bag

WHAT TO DO

1. Fill each Tic Tac box with a different spice.
2. Using an indelible marker, write the name of each spice on the clear plastic near the top of the box, using the white cap as the background. (Or use a label maker.)
3. Store the miniature spice boxes in a ziplock freezer bag.
4. To use, flip open the cap and sprinkle however much spice you desire.

HOW IT WORKS

Tic Tac containers hold a small amount of spice, and their snap-tight lids keep the spices sealed inside.

LOOKING HIGH AND LOW

You can also use Tic Tac boxes to hold:

- Beads
- Bobby pins
- Buttons
- DS game cartridges
- Fishing tackle
- Matches
- Paper clips
- Seeds
- Sewing kits
- Toothpicks
- Vitamins or pills

How to Open a Tin Can with a Concrete Block

WHAT YOU NEED
- Work gloves
- Safety goggles
- Sealed tin can
- Concrete block, sidewalk, or concrete slab

WHAT TO DO
1. Wearing work gloves and safety goggles, hold the sealed can upside down and rub the top in circles flat against the concrete until you grind down the rim.
2. Holding the can upright, gently squeeze the sides until the lid pops upward.

HOW IT WORKS
The top rim of the can is a crimp holding the top edge of the cylinder together with the lid. The friction created by rubbing the top edge of the tin can flat against the concrete erodes the crimp, loosening the lid.

OPENING A CAN OF WORMS
- In 1810, British merchant Peter Durand invented the metal can so he could supply rations to the Royal Navy. Unfortunately, Durand failed to invent a device to open the cans.
- During the War of 1812, British soldiers used pocketknives or bayonets to tear open canned rations—sometimes resorting to gunfire. The war popularized the metal can in England, despite the lack of an efficient can opener.

- Americans, while familiar with the metal can, had little use for it—until 1861 when soldiers fighting the Civil War needed preserved rations, necessitating canned foods.
- In 1858, Ezra J. Warner of Waterbury, Connecticut, invented and patented the first can opener—a fierce-looking device with a large curved blade like a sickle that the user stabbed into the can and then worked around the rim.
- In 1870, American inventor William W. Lyman developed a can opener with a cutting wheel that rolls around the rim of the can. In 1925, the Star Can Opener Company of San Francisco added a serrated "feed wheel" to Lyman's can opener so the can rotated against the wheel—the design used to this very day.
- On an arctic expedition in 1824, British explorer Sir William Parry carried a can of veal printed with the instructions, "Cut round on the top with a chisel and hammer."
- Some warfare historians claim that the bayonet was originally designed by a blacksmith in the French city of Bayonne as a can opener.

How to Prevent Campfire Soot on Pots and Pans with Soap

WHAT YOU NEED
- Pots and pans
- Bar of soap

WHAT TO DO
1. Before cooking over an open campfire, rub the bottoms of your pots and pans with a dry bar of soap to create a thin, waxy coating.
2. Leaving the soap in place on the pots and pans, use them for cooking.
3. After cooking, allow the pots and pans to cool to the touch, and then wash them with a scrubber.

HOW IT WORKS
The thin coat of soap enables you to wash black soot from the bottoms of the pots and pans effortlessly.

DIRTY WORK
- **Aluminum Foil.** A crumpled-up piece of aluminum foil makes an excellent pot scrubber to clean pots and pans used over a campfire grill.
- **Dishwashing Liquid.** If you don't have a bar of soap to rub on the bottoms of the pots and pans, coat the bottoms with a thin layer of dishwashing liquid. The black soot that forms on the bottom of the pots and pans wipes right off.
- **Shaving Cream.** No bar of soap? No dishwashing liquid? In a pinch, coat the bottoms of the pots and pans with shaving cream. Let the shaving cream dry before placing the cookware over the fire.

How to Uncork a Wine Bottle with a Shoe or Sneaker

WHAT YOU NEED
- Shoe or sneaker
- Solid wall or floor

WHAT TO DO
1. Remove the cap seal from the wine bottle.
2. Loosen the laces of the shoe or sneaker.
3. Insert the base of the wine bottle upright into the shoe or sneaker.
4. Holding both the wine bottle and the shoe or sneaker, bang the heel of the footwear against the wall or floor.
5. Repeat until the cork comes loose, then remove the cork by hand.

HOW IT WORKS
As Sir Isaac Newton's third law of motion states, for every action there is an opposite and equal reaction. Banging the bottom of the wine bottle against the wall forces the cork to move in the opposite direction, slowly prying itself from the neck of the bottle. The heel of the shoe or sneaker provides sufficient padding to prevent the glass bottle from breaking from the impact of the wall.

WINE AND DINE
- To chill wine more quickly than by putting the bottle on ice, pour the wine into a 1-gallon ziplock freezer bag and swirl around in a sink filled with ice water.
- There is no correlation between the price of a bottle of wine and its taste. Enjoy whatever wine appeals to you. Oftentimes, an inexpensive bottle of wine will taste better than an expensive bottle of wine.
- Wine connoisseurs tend to recommend dry white wines with fish, seafood, poultry, and light meats; pink rosé with all types of food; and robust red wines with red meat and game. However, you should drink whichever wine tastes best to you.

EVERY TRICK IN THE BOOK

Put a Cork in It

More ways to pop a cork from a wine bottle without a corkscrew:

- **Basketball Pump.** Insert the needle into the center of the cork and push down so the end of the needle penetrates the cork. Pump the air inside the bottle to increase the air pressure, popping the cork.
- **Book.** Instead of using a shoe or sneaker as illustrated on the previous page, use a book as the padding.
- **House Key.** Insert the key on a 45-degree angle all the way into the cork. Using the key, twist the cork clockwise while pushing upward, pulling out the cork.
- **Scissors.** Carefully insert the pointed blade of a pair of sharp scissors into the cork. Open the shear blade perpendicular to the pointed blade, and then carefully turn the handle of the shear blade clockwise while pushing the bottle downward, pulling out the cork.
- **Screw, Screwdriver, and Hammer.** Using a screwdriver, insert a screw into the center of the cork, leaving ½ inch of the screw exposed. Use the claw on the hammer to pull the screw (and the attached cork) from the bottle.
- **Screw Hook and Ballpoint Pen.** Insert a screw hook in the center of the cork, and then use a ballpoint pen as a T-bar to lift out the cork.

How to Solar Cook a Hot Dog with a Pringles Can

WHAT YOU NEED

- Hammer
- Nail
- Clean, empty Pringles potato chip can
- Indelible marker
- Ruler
- Utility knife or scissors
- Wooden skewer, 14 inches long
- Hot dog
- Clear packaging tape

WHAT TO DO

1. Using the hammer and nail, punch a small hole in the center of the metal bottom of a clean, empty Pringles can.

2. Remove the plastic lid from the can and use the hammer and nail to punch a hole in the center of the lid.

3. Using the indelible marker and ruler, draw a straight line along the length of the Pringles can.

4. Measure 1¼ inches from the bottom edge of the can along the length of the line, and draw a 3-inch line perpendicular to the length and bisected by the existing line.

5. Repeat step 2 measuring from the top edge of the can.

6. Using a utility knife or scissors, carefully cut the Pringles can as shown.

7. Fold back the two flaps.
8. Skewer the hot dog with the wooden skewer so that the hot dog is centered, slide the skewer into the can, and insert the end of the skewer into the hole in the metal end.
9. Place the plastic lid back onto the can, fitting the free end of the skewer through the hole so that the hot dog is suspended on the skewer inside the can and completely visible through the rectangular opening.
10. Cover the rectangular opening in the can with one or two strips of clear packaging tape to create a transparent window.
11. Place the solar cooker in direct sunlight, positioning the flaps to reflect the maximum amount of light onto the hot dog. Note that the angle at which the light hits the surface is equal to the angle at which it's reflected, the same way a flashlight beam is reflected off a mirror.
12. Let the solar cooker sit in the sun for 30 to 45 minutes.
13. Remove the hot dog from the can and skewer, and eat it.

HOW IT WORKS

The metallic flaps and interior of the can reflect, direct, and concentrate the radiant energy from the sun onto the hot dog. A portion of the concentrated radiant energy absorbed by the hot dog is converted into thermal energy (heat). The radiant energy passes through the window created by the clear packaging tape, but the window helps contain the thermal energy, cooking the hot dog faster than an open can.

EVERY TRICK IN THE BOOK

Jingle with Pringles

Some clever uses for a clean, empty Pringles can when traveling:

- **Store plastic bags.** Fill an empty Pringles can with the plastic shopping bags from stores, turning the can into a portable plastic bag dispenser.
- **Store yarn or string.** Run the yarn or string through a hole punched in the plastic lid of a Pringles can.
- **Pack paper cups, plasticware, and napkins for a picnic.** Five-ounce paper cups fit perfectly inside an empty Pringles can, as do paper napkins and plasticware.
- **Store pencils, pens, colored pencils, or crayons.** Use an empty Pringles can decorated with Con-Tact paper.
- **Store spaghetti.** A clean, empty Pringles can is just the right height to serve as an excellent airtight storage container for uncooked spaghetti. Cover with Con-Tact paper and label.
- **Store bread crumbs, flour, sugar, pasta, or biscuits.** Cover empty Pringles cans with Con-Tact paper and label.
- **Improvise a sick bag.** If you get motion sick, contain your mess in an empty Pringles can, replace the lid, and store until you can discard the can properly.
- **Pack jars of baby food for a trip.** An empty Pringles can hold three jars of Gerber baby food, protected by the paper padding.

Acknowledgments

At Chicago Review Press, I am grateful to my editor, Jerome Pohlen, for sharing my enthusiasm for this book and sharing his clever travel secrets with me. I am also deeply thankful to project editor Devon Freeny, designer Andrew Brozyna, my agent Laurie Abkemeier, researcher and photographer Debbie Green, photographer Julia Green, photographer Joanne Joyce, RV enthusiast Richard Primeau, and my manager Barb North. Above all, all my love to Debbie, Ashley, and Julia.

Bibliography

"Bend an Ear and Listen to the Tale of Vinegar" by Heloise. *Pittsburgh Press*, June 27, 1980.

"Birmingham Drug Mule Sparks Emergency Landing After £40,000 of Cocaine He Was Smuggling in His Stomach Burst on Packed Flight from Antigua" by *Daily Mail*. July 27, 2014.

"Charlie Parr's Guide to Cooking Under the Hood of Your Car" by Natalie Gallagher. *Minneapolis City Pages*, January 29, 2013.

"Cops Bust 21-Year-Old Female Drug Mule, Luisa Gill, with 50 condoms of cocaine in Her Stomach" by Philip Caulfield. *New York Daily News*, February 7, 2011.

"The Curious Walking Reeds of the Tijuana River" by Chad Deal. *San Diego Reader*, September 24, 2014.

"Dynamic Properties of Tennis Balls" by R. Cross. *Sports Engineering*, 1999, 23–33.

"Econundrum: 5 Handi-Wipes or Hot Shower?" by Kiera Butler. *Mother Jones*, January 25, 2010.

"8 Insider Secrets to Booking Cheap Airfare" by Daniel Bortz. *U.S. News and World Report*, April 18, 2012.

Emergency Food, Storage & Survival Handbook: Everything You Need to Know to Keep Your Family Safe in a Crisis by Peggy Layton. New York: Three Rivers Press, 2002.

"Five Myths About Germs on Aircraft" by Everett Potter. *USA Today*, October 13, 2014.

"Flatulence on Airplanes: Just Let It Go" by Hans C. Pommergaard, Jakob Burcharth, Anders Fischer, William E. G. Thomas, and Jacob Rosenberg. *New Zealand Medical Journal* 126, no. 1369 (February 15, 2013).

"Flight 93: Forty Lives, One Destiny" by Dennis B. Roddy with reporting from Cindi Lash, Steve Levin, and Jonathan D. Silver. *Pittsburgh Post-Gazette*, October 28, 2001.

The Formula Book by Norman Stark. New York: Avon, 1975.

"Going to the Laundrette—Delhi Style: Hundreds of Men Wash Clothes in One of the World's Most Polluted Rivers" by Julian Robinson. DailyMail.com, February 24, 2015, www.dailymail.co.uk/news /article-2967050/Going-laundrette-Delhi-style-Hundreds-men -wash-clothes-one-world-s-polluted-rivers.html.

"Halloween Costume Tips from 'Evil Dead: The Musical' Design Team" by Jenn McKee. *Ann Arbor News*, October 24, 2012.

"How Do I Fix a Dent in My Car?" by NewsCore. Fox News, June 22, 2012, www.foxnews.com/leisure/2012/06/22 /how-do-fix-dent-in-my-car/.

"How to Choose a Cabin" by Fran Golden. *USA Today*, June 26, 2013.

"How to Rack Up Frequent Flyer Miles" by Alexandra Talty. *Forbes*, November 26, 2013.

How to Survive Anything, Anywhere: A Handbook of Survival Skills for Every Scenario and Environment by Chris McNab. Camden, ME: McGraw-Hill, 2004.

How to Survive Anywhere: A Guide for Urban, Suburban, Rural, and Wilderness Environments by Christopher Nyerges. Mechanicsburg, PA: Stackpole Books, 2006.

"Intermediate Activity: Solar Cooking" by Energy Kids. US Energy Information Administration, www.eia.gov/kids/resources/teachers /pdfs/SolarCookingIntermediateActivity.pdf.

"Judge Denies Bail for Passenger Arrested After Fracas on Plane" by Sherri Day with Larry Rohter. *New York Times*, February 8, 2002.

"Kentucky Man Was Hiding Kilo of Cocaine in Lay's Potato Chip Bag, Foristell Police Say" by Susan Welch. *St. Louis Post-Dispatch*, October 28, 2014.

"Largest Collection of Sick Bags" by Guinness World Records. Official website, February 28, 2012, www.guinnessworldrecords.com /world-records/largest-collection-of-sick-bags.

"Long Night's Journey into Day" by Pete Hamill. *Rolling Stone*, June 5, 1975.

"Man Charged in Tennis Ball Bomb Case to Plead Guilty" by Kristine Guerra. *Indy Star*, November 17, 2014.

"Man Dies in Bid to Stop His Snoring" by *Herald Scotland*. March 9, 1996.

Manifold Destiny: The One! The Only! Guide to Cooking on Your Car Engine! by Bill Scheller and Chris Maynard. New York: Simon & Schuster, 2008.

"Members Only" by Mark Orwoll. *Travel + Leisure*, November 2011.

National Geographic Complete Survival Manual by Michael S. Sweeney. Washington, DC: National Geographic, 2009.

"Nick Cave's 'The Sick Bag Song,' an Epic Poem Composed on Tour" by Alexandra Alter. *New York Times*, April 17, 2015.

A Paranoid's Ultimate Survival Guide: Dust Mites to Meteorites, Tsunamis to Ticks, Killer Clouds to Jelly Fish, Solar Flares to Salmonella by Patricia Barnes-Svarney and Thomas Eugene Svarney. Amherst, NY: Prometheus Books, 2002.

Periods in Pop Culture: Menstruation in Film and Television by Lauren Rosewarne. Lanham, MD: Lexington Books, 2012.

"Photo in the News: Python Undergoes Golf Ball-ectomy" by Ted Chamberlain. National Geographic News, January 3, 2007, http://news.nationalgeographic.com/news/2008/01/080103-snakes-picture.html.

"Pool Noodle Duel Between Self-Styled Inventors Dates Back 30 Years" by Alex Ballingall. *Toronto Star*, June 28, 2014.

"Putting Myself Together" by Jamaica Kincaid. *New Yorker*, February 20, 1995, 93.

"Reflecting on Space Benefits: A Shining Example" by NASA. *Spinoff*, September 2006.

Re/Uses: 2,133 Ways to Recycle and Reuse the Things You Ordinarily Throw Away by Carolyn Jabs. New York: Crown, 1982.

"'Sleep Was My Enemy': A Bond Actress on Battling Insomnia" by Christine Fieldhouse. *Express*, August 5, 2014.

Special Forces Survival Guide: Wilderness Survival Skills from the World's Most Elite Military Units by Chris McNab. Berkeley, CA: Ulysses, 2008.

Stay Alive!: Survival Skills You Need by John D. McCann. Iola, WI: Krause Publications, 2011.

Survival by Hugh C. McDonald. New York: Ballantine Books, 1982.

The Ultimate Survival Manual: 333 Skills That Will Get You Out Alive by Rich Johnson and the editors of *Outdoor Life*. San Francisco: Weldon Owen, 2012.

"Unlocking a Car with Your Brain" by Roger Bowley. Sixty Symbols, March 17, 2014, www.youtube.com/watch?v=0Uqf71muwWc.

Vinegar, Duct Tape, Milk Jugs & More: 1,001 Ingenious Ways to Use Common Household Items to Repair, Restore, Revive, or Replace Just about Everything in Your Life by Earl Proulx and the editors of *Yankee Magazine*. Emmaus, PA: Rodale, 1999.

"Why Burger King Gave These Funny Sleep Masks to Korean Commuters" by Angela Doland. *Advertising Age*, April 22, 2015.

You Only Die Once by Margie Little Jenkins. Brentwood, TN: Integrity, 2002.

About Joey Green

Joey Green is a walking encyclopedia of quirky yet ingenious household hints. A former contributing editor to *National Lampoon* and a former advertising copywriter at J. Walter Thompson, Joey has written television commercials for Burger King and Walt Disney World, and he won a Clio for a print ad he created for Eastman Kodak before launching his career as a bestselling author. Joey has appeared on dozens of national television shows, including *The Tonight Show with Jay Leno*, *Good Morning America*, and *The View*. He has been profiled in the *New York Times*, *People*, the *Los Angeles Times*, the *Washington Post*, and *USA Today*, and he has been interviewed on hundreds of radio shows.

A native of Miami, Florida, and a graduate of Cornell University (where he founded the campus humor magazine, the *Cornell Lunatic*, still publishing to this very day), he lives in Los Angeles.

Other Books by Joey Green

- *Last-Minute Survival Secrets*
- *Happy Accidents*
- *Contrary to Popular Belief*
- *Joey Green's Cleaning Magic*
- *Joey Green's Amazing Pet Cures*
- *Joey Green's Magic Health Remedies*
- *Weird & Wonderful Christmas*
- *The Ultimate Mad Scientist Handbook*
- *Joey Green's Kitchen Magic*
- *Dumb History: The Stupidest Mistakes Ever Made*

- *Selling Out: If Famous Authors Wrote Advertising*
- *Joey Green's Fix-It Magic*
- *Joey Green's Gardening Magic*
- *You Know You've Reached Middle Age If . . .*
- *Clean It! Fix It! Eat It!*
- *Marx & Lennon: The Parallel Sayings*
- *Too Old for MySpace, Too Young for Medicare*